T0158810

BECOMING LOVE
ON FIRE, TO LEAD

LEAD LIKE THE SUN

MICHELLE COCHRAN

WESTBOW
PRESS®
A DIVISION OF THOMAS NELSON
& ZONDERVAN

This book is a work of non-fiction. Unless otherwise noted, the author and the publisher make no explicit guarantees as to the accuracy of the information contained in this book and in some cases, names of people and places have been altered to protect their privacy.

Scripture taken from the New King James Version. Copyright © 1979, 1980, 1982 by Thomas Nelson, Inc. Used by permission. All rights reserved.

Scripture taken from the Holy Bible, NEW INTERNATIONAL VERSION®. Copyright © 1973, 1978, 1984, 2011 by Biblica, Inc. All rights reserved worldwide. Used by permission. NEW INTERNATIONAL VERSION® and NIV® are registered trademarks of Biblica, Inc. Use of either trademark for the offering of goods or services requires the prior written consent of Biblica US, Inc.

All Scripture quotations in this publications are from The Message. Copyright © by Eugene H. Peterson 1993, 1994, 1995, 1996, 2000, 2001, 2002. Used by permission of NavPress Publishing Group.

Scripture quotations are from The Holy Bible, English Standard Version® (ESV®), copyright © 2001 by Crossway, a publishing ministry of Good News Publishers. Used by permission. All rights reserved.

Scripture quotations taken from the Holy Bible, New Living Translation, Copyright © 1996, 2004. Used by permission of Tyndale House Publishers, Inc., Wheaton, Illinois 60189. All rights reserved.

Scripture taken from the Holman Christian Standard Bible ® Copyright © 2003, 2002, 2000, 1999 by Holman Bible Publishers. All rights reserved.

Scripture taken from the Holy Bible: International Standard Version® Release 2.0. Copyright © 1996-2012 by the ISV Foundation. ALL RIGHTS RESERVED INTERNATIONALLY.

Scripture quotations are from The Holy Bible, English Standard Version® (ESV®), copyright © 2001 by Crossway, a publishing ministry of Good News Publishers. Used by permission. All rights reserved.

WestBow Press books may be ordered through booksellers or by contacting:

WestBow Press
A Division of Thomas Nelson & Zondervan
1663 Liberty Drive
Bloomington, IN 47403
www.westbowpress.com
1 (866) 928-1240

Because of the dynamic nature of the Internet, any web addresses or links contained in this book may have changed since publication and may no longer be valid. The views expressed in this work are solely those of the author and do not necessarily reflect the views of the publisher, and the publisher hereby disclaims any responsibility for them.

Any people depicted in stock imagery provided by Thinkstock are models, and such images are being used for illustrative purposes only. Certain stock imagery © Thinkstock.

ISBN: 978-1-5127-5006-5 (sc)
ISBN: 978-1-5127-5007-2 (hc)
ISBN: 978-1-5127-5005-8 (e)

Library of Congress Control Number: 2016911906

Print information available on the last page.

WestBow Press rev. date: 09/29/2016

"But let those who love Him be like the sun when it comes out in full strength."

Judges 5:31 (NKJV)

Contents

Breaths Of Fresh Air

Have you ever taken a walk on the beach, when the sand was really hot on your feet, the sun was beating down, and the noises of summer buzzed all around you? Even though it is fun and enjoyable, in that moment, you long for just a little hint of refreshment. Then all of a sudden a sweet breeze blows gently across the water and you can't help but say, "Aaaahhhh," right out loud.

There are some people God has written into my life story that have been that sweet breeze blowing into my life and work, and I must acknowledge them. Each one of these amazing individuals have been such a breath of fresh air to me they make me say, "Aaaahhhh," right out loud.

Jesus - My dear sweet amazing Jesus; the reason I live, draw breath, or do anything. I love you desperately, whole-heartedly, and pray you will continue to teach me how to love you more every day. You truly are everything and I adore you. Thank you for Yourself, salvation, healing, redemption, faith, love, grace, mercy and your presence. Thank you for leading me to write this book. I pray you will bless everyone who reads it with whatever you intend for them to take away. And may your grace, love, and mercy follow them all the days of their lives.

Mark Cochran - My husband, my best friend, my love. With you I often see myself as a balloon with a really long string, wanting to float off in every direction and dream I feel called to follow. You are the 'paper-weight' to my really long string, keeping me grounded and safe. You love me, support and encourage me, and I am forever grateful God gave us to each other. Thank you for putting up with me while I figured this all out, and for never giving up on me. Even during those really ugly bouts of crying and messy meltdowns. God has made you strong and courageous and I love you.

Justin, Jacob, & Markie - My children and my heart. Wow, God has made each of you so different, you are fearfully and wonderfully made!

As your mom I could go on for days and pages about who you are and how I love you. But I just thank God that He let me be your mom. I once heard a quote about how looking at your kids is like seeing your heart walk around outside your body. That is so true. Each one of you has brought a different blessing, teaching, and love to my life. I love you all so much, and more than anything I pray that you love Jesus with all your heart, soul, mind, and strength.

Crissie Bacon - My true-blue, sister-friend. You are the longest, best, loyal, constant friend. I have broken the most rules and laughed the hardest with you. You challenge me, you keep life really real, you ask the tough questions. You are generous with your heart, time, and talents. You are an amazing cook, funny, and strong. You are a sister in Christ and in my heart. God blessed me with your friendship and you are my forever friend and family. I love you.

Nancy Rizzo - My dear coaching buddy and 'Nanner.' You have walked with me through so much change and growth. And you are a huge reason why I emerged even half sane from it. God made us 'bookends' in this life, each of our lives parallel and encompassing so much of the same 'stuff.' You crack me up, you help me keep it simple, you are smart and sassy, and a gift from above! Everyone needs a 'Nanner,' Especially me! I love you and wish you every blessing from heaven, as you continue to change lives with whom He has made you.

Gayle Page - My sunshine friend. Thank you for inviting me to bible study. You are a constant ray of light. God brought us together in a divine appointment that allowed us both to move forward in Him. I will be forever grateful for that special time in our lives and your friendship. You have a sweet and tender place in my heart, I love you.

Valerie Hunsberger - Whose name I can barely even type without crying. Half of this book could be filled with all the things I have learned thanks to you. And all the things you mean to me because of how God has used you in my life. You are a mentor, a light, a joy, a blessing, a teacher, a sister, a friend. "Thank you and I love you" they do not seem enough. You have given so much of yourself to me they don't begin to cover how I feel about you. Your heart is so full of Jesus and you are a powerful, radiant, example of what it is to follow and love Him. My hope, as one discipled by you, is to do work worthy of the effort you put into me. May God bless you abundantly with His presence, love, and blessings. When I grow up I want to be just like you.

Carol Greer - Oh sistah, my sistah. It may be your ringtone for me but it also speaks volumes about who you are to me. You are a sweet sister in Christ who is a constant encouragement and light. You have a dear simple love for Jesus that let's you speak it so well, and you inspire me! You listen and love so well and God has blessed me with the gift of your heart and ears so many times. I am grateful to walk this journey of love for Jesus together. He has given us adventures and lots of laughs, thank you, my dear friend, I love you.

Danielle Bivens - God brought us together at a time when the spirit was moving in new and thrilling ways in our lives. You are constant wisdom and joy, always seeking God's heart and will. I have experienced things with you that I haven't with any other friend or sister and you are near and dear to my heart. I love the mother, professional, and light that you are. I am so blessed that God crossed our paths and to call you my sister in Christ.

Heidi Mclane - My freedom sister. We are still figuring out all the awesome reasons God has caused our paths to cross. But I am so glad He did cross them! You are smart, so funny, and a highly effective teacher. You challenge me spiritually, intellectually, and you make me laugh so hard I wheez...not an easy feat to accomplish. I can't wait to see all that God has in store for you. You are a teacher, a seeker of God and knowledge, and a lover of mazy and Josie (your sweet doggies). Who wouldn't love being with you? You bring truth, authenticity, and speak freedom to everyone you are blessed to. Thank you for speaking and being it to me, I love who you are and how God uses you.

Tracy Collier - My pastor, sister, editor, and friend. Oh the light that you are! You have a heart that chases down the heart of God. It manifests in love and excellence in all that you do. It challenges those of us blessed to walk with you. It holds a space of hope, joy, and love. This book would not have reached publication if God had not given me you. Thank you for all of your precious time, listening, praying, encouraging, and working so hard to make this book dream a reality. I love you and I am so excited for our next chapter in Jesus together!

Jane Robinson - My sister of art and moxy. You remind me to be creative. Your style and moxy make me smile and bring me so much joy. I love your heart for God and making a difference in the lives around you. Thank you for being on the 'artrepreneurial' path with me, for talking about our dreams, and a life well lived and spent. You are generous, sacrificial, and incredibly kind. You bring a spark to my heart and my day, I'm so lucky to know you. I pray God's presence and blessings on you and your family. You are an inspiration and I love you.

Teresa Snijder - My sister, my friend. You are an awesome woman and mom. You are so smart and one of the funniest people I know. Thank you for being such a good sister to me. God has put a very tender and special place in my heart for you. I love you so much.

A special thank you to Stephanie Collier and Karen Muse for their expertise, kindness, and generosity.

Foreword

Dear Friend Reader,

It's no accident that you have chosen this book. I believe God has led you here to begin a journey of healing and joy and peace. I believe this because I have prayed for you. Not by name of course. But I and others, including our soon-to-be mutual friend, Michelle Cochran, have prayed that the Lord would use this book to bring hope and restoration to your life.

So let me tell you a little about my friend! I won't take long because I don't want to delay you on your journey. I met Michelle during a class I teach about spiritual gifts and ministry passion. And we discovered that she is passionate about you! Again, maybe not by name, but in a way that encourages healing and wholeness in the Lord, for all women. That's you!

I am privileged to call Michelle Cochran my friend and sister in Christ. I trust her implicitly and have experienced firsthand her devotion to God and the fruit of it in her ministry. She even let me help with her first edit and write this letter to you. She's pretty great! But her greatness comes from a deep love for the Lord and a heart turned toward His will.

Be encouraged. We will continue to pray for you. Some of this journey may be difficult or even painful, but I believe you are about to become closer to Jesus than you have ever been. And that is so worth it!

Read on, dear friend. Enjoy the journey. Know that you may have to go over these "paths' more than once, but that's okay. Take your time. You are worth it!

Love in Christ,

Tracy L. Collier
Ministry Placement & Community Groups Pastor
First Church of the Nazarene, Jackson, MI
July 1, 2015

Introduction

For Women Called To The Warrior Faction In Jesus:

"You shall love the Lord your God with all your heart, and with all your soul, and with all your strength, and with all your mind; and your neighbor as yourself."

- Luke 10:27 (AKJV)

There is a battle raging for the souls of the next generation and the lives of every man, woman, and child. It's a spiritual battle and therefore we must fight like it. Love is our most powerful weapon.

God is advancing His Kingdom, and as daughters of the King, we are equipped to arise, radiate, and reign on this earth.

The sun burns at its core at about 27 million degrees. Deborah, a wise woman of her time, called to lead in battle, sang in her victory song: "But let those who love Him be like the sun, when it comes out in full strength.

(Judges 5:31 NKJV)

What an interesting and beautiful analogy she sings to us in her moment of triumph, after a tough battle. Meditate on that for just a moment, a calling, winning, and the sun out in full strength. The correlation is a radiant, bold, love that burns within, and what it can cause us to do and become, because we love Him.

Dare I say our love for Jesus burns hotter than 27 million degrees at our core! And we will never be more effective than when we let that come out in full strength! The question is: Are you willing to come out in full and vibrant strength as a light, and as an individual? Rising up, radiating His love and power inside you, in faith and full expression? That is how this battle is fought and won.

We are set as a light, just like Jesus, as a sign, a wonder, a guide, to hold back darkness, being for salvation to the ends of the earth.

"That He would be the first to rise from the dead, and would proclaim light to the Jewish and Gentile people."
                                            - Acts 26:23 (NKJV)

"For so the Lord has commanded us; I have set you as a light to the Gentiles, that you should be for salvation to the ends of the earth."
                                            - Acts 13:47 (NKJV)

These verses are from the book of Acts in the Bible, which is a book of mess, transition, and miracles. At that time people were afraid, skeptical, and desperate. Desperate to hold onto the old because it was all they had known or maybe wanted to know.

But God was pouring out His spirit on a newly forming church and using it to do works in and through people.

Just like in the book of Acts, I believe that God is doing a new thing in and through women. I believe He is calling women to lead radiantly and effectively where they are, and in who He is making them. When God does a new thing He pours His spirit out on His people to achieve His purposes and it's messy. There is no "road map" and those called to lead are going first in new and different ways. They're willing, like Deborah, because they love Him. But it's uncertain and requires strength, bravery, and a wide open heart. Also, just like in Acts, the old and the new collide and everyone freaks out because we don't deal with change very well. But God is summoning His warriors, preparing them for battle, and we must choose. Will we cling to earthly securities or fling wide our hearts and efforts to love a desperate world?

Even the Israelites were willing to go back into Egypt, into slavery, to maintain their earthly sense of security when God was leading them to the promised land. These events happened a long time ago, but the God that was leading them then, is still leading us now. He does things His way, and we still argue, and struggle, history repeats itself.

But as wise women of God, who hear, who see, and know He is calling us out of our earthly bondages to be set as a light to the gentiles, and to prepare the way for His return. We can see the darkness amping up its efforts, its time is short. Therefore, as the light of the world, it is our time as well. It is our time lead, to be brave and willing to let go of some old, step into some new, and be the difference in the darkness.

Jesus literally came to me as light as I laid in a bed wishing for death. He caused me to rise, and taught me some things about living free in Him, walking in faith, and leading in full strength and expression of His love for and in me.

I believe He taught me those things for such a time as this, a time for bravery and ownership of our individual stories. A time for courageous expression of them, and a time to collectively impact a world in need of more light, with them.

I see and hear women from all walks of life, gifting, and professions who know they are called to step up, speak up, and make their difference. But hold themselves back in various forms of fear and insecurities. I know because I have lived most of them.

Ladies, the gauntlet has been thrown down, and you are a warrior in Jesus. No more hiding, no more waiting to get it all right, no more worrying about what other people will say or do. Although we seek the wise counsel of many, we obey and take our marching orders from God, and God alone.

It is time to throw off all that hinders, and to rise above circumstance, oppression, and status quo. To walk in confident freedom, and lead as light, in a world that desperately needs more and stronger light.

As individuals, we love Jesus, and He is the light in us and at the end of our paths. As we walk toward Him, His light in and through us becomes stronger, brighter, and more effective. So that we can lead the way for another sister who may be stuck in the wilderness, looking for a ray of hope, back to her God-given path of glory and effectiveness.

Collectively, we will flood the earth with the light of His glory. Until the day the Light of the world Himself returns and we sing, "Holy, holy, holy, is the Lord God Almighty!" with tears of joy streaking our faces and hearts ablaze, for the One who made it all so very worth it!

Isn't that what we want to know, that in the end, if nothing else, our poured out hearts and efforts were so very worth it? Sisters, I believe not only is it worth it, but that it is all there is. He proved it as He hung on the cross, that a life poured out as light for love is what it's all about. And how we fight the good fight of faith.

Our work is to believe Him. I am praying for you, your heart, your peace, courage, and an emboldened relationship with Jesus. That you will be an even more effective light, for the building up of His Kingdom, and the saving of souls.

This book is my personal experience and expression with how God taught me to Lead Like The Sun, when it comes out in full strength, thus far. I hope it blesses and encourages you. You'll find stories, along with 'coaching pieces' within different topics, that support the over-arching idea of being effective light.

One thing I am certain of, like Deborah, we've got the victory! All we have to do is burn and shine, letting the world see His glory in us.

Let's let our victory cry be "Yes Lord!" whatever He calls us out of or to. Let us throw up our hands in confidence that He has our front, side, and back. Let's walk with contrite hearts and willing and adventurous spirits. For He is our God, and we are His people, warriors of audacious love and light. So for the joy set before us, let us lead like the sun, and the Son.

The Light Of Dawn

"The people who sat in darkness have seen a great light. And for those who lived in the land where death casts its shadow, a light has shined."

- Matthew 4:16 (NLT)

I stood in the kitchen of what was my best friend's house. I had been living with her, her sister, and mother for over a year; I was sixteen years old. Chaos, abuse, and neglect had brought me to live there, and they had graciously accepted me. I was in high school. Anyone who has been through high school knows how cruel kids can be with teasing and pressure. My friend was being targeted with constant taunting about she and I living in the same house.

One night, her mother, so soft-spoken and gentle in nature, called me into the kitchen. She told me that my friend could no longer have me there and that I needed to leave right away.

It felt slow-motion surreal like in the movies, and I am sure it would have hurt much less if she had just punched me in the stomach. My mind raced a million miles a second, with shock and questions. What is she saying? What is happening? Does she know I have no where to go? Why would my friend do this to me? Why isn't she telling me herself? What did I do?

As I snapped back into consciousness, I heard her end her sentence with, "I'm sorry, but you just need to go." I was shocked and devastated. I grabbed my car keys and headed for my rusted out Datsun B210. It was given to me as a gift by grandparents, as they too had fled the chaos that was my mother's life, and moved to Florida.

It was pouring down rain, by the time I got into the car I was soaking wet. The rain drops smacked the windshield hard and my wipers could not keep up. I could barely see through my tears and the windshield to drive, and I had no idea where I was going. I just drove. My chest heaved as I cried and I tried to make sense of what was happening, and why life was so hard. I thought, 'what the heck is going on, I am sixteen years old and it seems all I do is fight. Fight to survive, fight for my sanity, fight for place to live, to eat, fight for safety and protection, for everything.'

I sobbed I was so tired, so angry, so frustrated, so alone, and so incredibly hopeless.

When my car came to a stop I looked up through the rain-drenched windshield, with the wipers lapping furiously back and forth. I was looking at the cemetery that was at the end of my grandparents old street. I cried out to God and said, "Take my life I can't do this anymore, I am done fighting, so either you take my life right now or show me how!"

Even now my heart sinks and my keyboard is dotted with tears, reliving that moment. I was so tired, hopeless, and so angry at

God. I knew He was there, but why was He doing this to me, and what on earth was I going to do?

I drove back to my friends house and fell into bed worn out. The next morning I vividly remember the actual parting of my eyelids, my eyes opening. I thought, 'Well He didn't kill me so maybe He is going to show me how.' So I got up. I found a newspaper to see if by chance there was a place for rent that I could afford. I was working three jobs while finishing high school.

I found a studio apartment in the upper part of a house, on the bad side of town, on Seymour Street. They were asking $200.00 per month and I thought maybe I could afford that, so I called, and a man answered. I told him I was interested in his place and asked if I could I please take a look at it. He agreed.

I wish you could have seen his face when he got out of his car, and there in his driveway, stood a sixteen year old girl. For whatever reason, he went ahead with the apartment showing. It had been recently fixed up, was clean, and even a little cute, but very small. I knew I wanted to rent the place and mustered the courage to ask him. When I did ask he paused. I could see that he was sizing me up in his mind.

I said, "Sir, I know that I am young, but if you will just take a chance on me, I will take care of your place and I will pay my rent on time, I promise." He thought a moment, and then he agreed, to my surprise and relief.

I moved in with the remnants of what friends gave me in the way of furniture, including a twin bed. I was relieved to have a place I could call my own, but scared to death of being there alone at night. I desperately wanted to have a phone so if I did have problems I could call for help. This is back when phones were still mostly on walls. I scrimped and saved until I finally had enough money to get a phone.

I was so excited and relieved. I went to the neighbors house and asked if I could use their phone to call the phone company, which they let me do. When the lady at the phone company answered, I told her I would like to get a phone turned on at my address. She asked the particulars; my name, social security number, and address, and then there was a pause.

I wondered what was taking so long, when suddenly she said, "Um, I'm afraid I can't turn a phone on in your name, you have an outstanding bill of $500.00."

I instantly retorted, "What? I can't have a $500 phone bill, I have never had a phone in my name before?" The words no sooner left my mouth and my heart sank into my stomach. I thought I would be sick. I knew instantly that my mother had used my social security number to get a phone, and didn't pay the bill. Desperate people do desperate things, and she was frequently desperate.

I was sick, sad, hurt, and so embarrassed and I said, "Ma'am, I'm so sorry. I think I know what happened. I think someone may have used my social security number and didn't pay the bill."

She said, "Hold on a moment."

As I sat on hold I wondered how on earth I was going to come up with $500.00 to pay this bill, certain that was my fate. She came back on the line and I braced myself.

She said, "Honey, I have taken care of that for you, here is your new number."

I was confused and relieved. I wrote down the new number as quick as I could. I thanked her, hung up the phone, and put my head down on that neighbors kitchen table and cried. What was this generosity, this grace? I surely did not recognize it. But I was grateful and all I could do was cry.

One night, after the Datsun B210 engine seized up, (because the grandparents failed to mention that you put oil in car). I was walking home from work. It was about 9:30 p.m. and in my new neighborhood I walked quickly and very alert. As I rounded the back side of the house that my apartment was in, I could sense someone on the deck at my front door.

I was terrified, I backed way up so I could see who was there. It was my mother. She had just been released from jail after some petty crimes and had heard I was living there. She had no where to go she told me, and wondered if she could please stay with me for a while.

Of course I said yes. With the understanding that she would be sleeping on a couch that had several springs sticking out in various places. She didn't seem to mind, as she was once again, desperate.

I continued to work and go to school. I loved school. First I loved to learn, but more importantly at that time, school was my sense of security. It was my one constant and home, where the people and rules stayed pretty much the same. But I was living out of the district and it was very difficult to get there everyday. I was always bumming rides off of friends, taking the city bus, walking, whatever it took to get there. I knew without a high school diploma, I wouldn't amount to anything in this life, and I was determined to finish.

After a month or two my mom found her own apartment in another house on the same bad side of town. About a month after that, my lease was up, and it seemed so was I. I found myself not only emotionally exhausted, but now physically exhausted.

I called my mom and told her that I needed to come and stay with her for a while, and she said okay. She had a one bedroom apartment with one double bed, I didn't care, I just needed a place to rest. I crawled into that double bed and for almost three weeks I didn't get out. Except maybe to use the ladies room or have a hint of food.

The powder blue sheets became moist and clammy from too much use, and I started to smell really bad. I thought if I just kept laying there eventually I'd have to die. It seemed medically and physically impossible that a human could maintain this and not die. I wanted out. Out of this life, this impossible, mean, scary, ugly, cruel life and I was going to lay there until it happened. I was convinced that no one could or would ever really love me. Not like "poor me" no one will love me, but utterly convinced of the truth that people weren't capable of it. And maybe I wasn't worthy of it either.

One morning, I again remember my eyelids physically parting. I opened my eyes and grimaced at the reality that they had indeed opened again. As I begrudgingly rolled over, I saw a beam of sunlight that had somehow managed to skirt around the drawn shade, where it didn't quite meet the window frame. I thought, 'How did that get in here?'

But as I looked at it, I was mesmerized. It seemed to have electricity in it, pulsating with dancing threads of orange, green, and various shades of white and yellow. I thought, 'Well that's weird, ya don't see that everyday.' I couldn't stop staring at it. It felt alive and I was awestruck, watching it flicker, when I heard a voice in my spirit say, "Get up."

In my true strong-willed nature I rebutted, "NO, I'm not getting up! It's hard out there, and mean, and scary and I don't want to do it anymore!"

There was a brief pause, and again I heard, "Get up." To which I stood my ground and replied, "No, I'm not getting up."

A door was all that separated the living room and the bedroom where I lay arguing. Just then, I heard my mother who was on the phone, laugh.

I don't mean, chuckle, chuckle ha, ha laugh. I mean full on belly laugh. Something rose up in me and before I knew it I was hurling back the clammy covers and sitting on the edge of the bed.

All I could think after hearing her laugh was, you let me lay here for almost 3 weeks, and you are belly laughing??!!!! I thought, 'Oh no you didn't,' and I flew into the shower. I got cleaned up, found a ride to school, and went in to plead my case. Because I had missed so many days, and it was my senior year. My education meant everything to me, and I knew I was again going to have to fight for it. But this time, it wasn't me doing the fighting. Something in me was moving me.

I got to the school and asked to meet with the principal. Since I had worked as an office aide, they knew me, and were willing to get me right in. I had spent my life to this point hiding the truth of my circumstances from those at school the best I could. Always putting on a smile, an excellent front of 'all is well,' and I am an achiever!

This meeting was going to be painful. I was going to have to be open and completely honest for the very first time. That kind of vulnerability was terrifying to me.

The principal came in and greeted me as he took his seat on the other side of the desk. He asked, "How can I help you today?" I could feel my face draining of all color, and there was no air in my lungs for a moment. But I drew a deep breath and began spilling my heart and soul about where I had been, and why I had been there. Even about memories of sexual abuse that came flooding back that I had no idea what to do with. Who just blurts that out in a 'can I come back to school meeting?' But once the floodgates opened my soul poured out. I was now desperate. Desperate for forgiveness, for acceptance, and to finish school and get my diploma.

And as he gazed across the desk at me he said, "I'm sorry, you have just missed too many days."

I began to beg him, I pleaded, "Sir, I will do whatever it takes to graduate on time and with my friends. I will do extra credit work. I will stay after school every day to make up time or work. I will do whatever it takes please, please let me finish."

He said, "I'm sorry, you have missed too many days."

I felt like he had reached in my chest, pulled my heart out, and stomped on it. I also felt in that moment something rise up in me again. I knew I had to make a choice about what to do with this answer. I stood up, thanked him for his time, and left. I went immediately to another school district and I signed up for summer school. I never missed a day. I graduated high school with a 4.0 and honors, ironically in psychology.

I would like to tell you that from there I got with Jesus and it was smooth sailing. But I had developed quite a self-reliant will with a thick skull. I believed that even though God was there, I still had to do it all myself. I will share more details about that later. But suffice it to say my path zigged and zagged, as I sought to fulfill a yearning in me I could not name. I was carrying with me, a heap of hurt and deep wounds, that consistently told me how unworthy and not good enough I was.

Looking back on that time in my life. I always knew God had used it to help me grow stronger and teach me about His love and sovereignty. But never in my wildest dreams did I believe He could actually redeem and use it. I was quite happy leaving all of that behind me, even pretending at times it didn't happen. But He is so good, such a "full circle" God. There is nothing He can't use for His purposes. He made me a fighter. He taught me how to fight a good fight of faith and perseverance.

As I look at our current times and circumstances. He is making very apparent to me the amount of people that are called to fight the good fight. And God is authoring it through them. But many are in what was my kind of bondage, oppression, and 'regions and shadows of death,' as the verse above says. And it burdens my heart. Some days I don't know whether to get fired up and yell, or bawl my eyes out. I hate oppression in any form, hate it. I can't tolerate it for me, or for any other women God is calling up and out.

That's why I believe God is using this sunbeam story; Him coming to me as light and calling me to "Get up." It is to help other women rise, radiate, and lead the same way He has taught me, and for such a time as this.

The world needs more light and you are it. The beautifully ordinary girl with a heart and vision that can change everything right where you are. As you let God raise you up and you radiate His presence.

Today, I love sunbeams in the morning as they grace my walls or spread across my floor, dancing with vibrant life. To me, they are kisses from God. A reminder from Him that He loves me, and is with me, as much now as He was then. Only now, I know that dancing, vibrant, resurrecting light is on the inside of me. And if you are following Jesus, it is on the inside of you.

So what will we do with it? Will we hide it? Keep it to ourselves in fear and insecurities? Be deterred by religious baggage or status quo? If you are holding a book of this title, you know it is time for you to rise, radiate, and reign with whatever the love dancing inside of you looks like.

What I learned better than anything else from my youth was to fight for the better story God was authoring as my life, and to lead as an individual in it. We, as the light in the world, must learn to lead as individuals, together. One sun, one Son, and one girl on fire for a world He came to save.

Deborah sang in her victory song: "Village life ceased, it ceased in Israel, Until I, Deborah, arose." - Judges 5:7 (NKJV)

Until I, (insert your name here)_____

_____, arose!

Isaiah 60:1-7 (Msg)

Get out of bed, Jerusalem!
Wake up. Put your face in the sunlight.
God's bright glory has risen for you.
The whole earth is wrapped in darkness,
all people sunk in deep darkness,
But God rises on you,
His sunrise glory breaks over you.
Nations will come to your light,
Kings to your sunburst brightness.
Look up! Look around!
Watch as they gather, watch as they approach you:
Your sons coming from great distances,
your daughters carried by their nannies.
When you see them coming you'll smile—big smiles!
Your heart will swell and, yes, burst!

What happens when the love of God shines through you, like the sun in full strength?

It changes and leads, everything and everyone, including you.

Let us think of ways to motivate one another to acts of love and good works. And let us not neglect our meeting together, as some people do, but encourage one another, especially now that the day of his return is drawing near.

- Hebrews 10:24-25 (NLT)

Love.

Love Moves.

Love Gives.

Love Strengthens.

Love Serves.

Love Heals.

Love Opens.

Love Lifts.

Love Frees.

Love Empowers.

Love Is God.

Learn to Lead, Lead to Love.

"We must grow strong enough to love & love enough to lead."

- Michelle Cochran

There are only three questions you ever need to ask to determine how to lead to love:

1) Knowing the definition of 'agape' to be: (according to dictionary.com) with mouth wide open, as in wonder, surprise, or eagerness. It is a sacrificial, selfless, supernatural love, described as the highest form of the four kinds of love found in the Bible. Ask yourself; how does the Father love me?

_____
_____
_____
_____
_____
_____
_____
_____
_____
_____
_____
_____

2) How do I love the Father?

_____
_____
_____
_____
_____
_____
_____
_____
_____
_____
_____
_____

3) What does that love want me to do to help or contribute?

_____
_____

_____

_____

_____

_____

_____

_____

_____

_____

_____

When our hearts are set and aligned with the love of the Father, there comes an illumination of the spirit, that leads naturally.

There is nothing more perfect or powerful than the love of God. It is our fuel, our identity, and our purpose, as Christ followers and as leaders. Our work is to intentionally and effectively share and serve in the love of Christ Jesus, in faith and full expression!

This isn't a new message really, but one that needs to be believed, owned, and acted upon radically, at this time on the Kingdom calendar. Just imagine the adventure, the joy, the nearness to God, in the sheer audacity to live and lead from a place where you choose to do ALL things through Christ, who loves you and will strengthen you!

Do everything in love, with love, and for love and you will lead like the Son and the sun. A brilliant light bringing hope, in a world desperately looking for more light and hope. Nothing less than this will satisfy the girl who knows her Father is causing her to burn with love for Him and is ready and willing to obediently express it.

WATCH THE ACCOMPANYING VIDEO
AT STRONGGIRLPRODUCTIONS.COM

Arise

"Talitha Cumi"
"little girl, I say to you Arise!" - *Jesus*

- Mark 5:41 NKJV

Jesus spoke these words to the daughter of a synagogue leader whom had died: "Talitha Cumi," which in Aramaic means 'little girl, I say to you arise.' Today He bids you, "Talitha Cumi!" Arise this day and choose whom you will serve, live, and fight for.

Isaiah 60 (NKJV)

Arise, shine;
For your light has come!
And the glory of the Lord is risen upon you.
For behold, the darkness shall cover the earth,
And deep darkness the people;
But the Lord will arise over you,
And His glory will be seen upon you.

Did you know that the word, "Arise," is used 158 times in the bible (NKJV)? It carries weight, authority, and purpose. The

definition, according to The King James Bible Page is - Arise://
To emerge from below the horizon; as, the sun or a star arises or
rises; to begin to act; to exert power.

Well, we certainly know of one incredible rising from below the
horizon and exertion of power. Our Lord Jesus Christ rose from
the grave, conquering death itself, and rose or ascended to the
right hand of God.

The knowing of this is our hope and the reason for our faith. The
power of it lives inside of us! That's a whole lot of rising power!

Like the sun cresting the morning horizon, bringing hope and
life anew, God has raised you up as light, and prepared you for
battle. Have you ever tried to stare directly at the sun, or imagine
being next to it? You wouldn't stand much of a chance against
its radiant power. Nor will anything or anyone that might come
against you, stand a chance!

It is time for you to rise and shine, for the glory of the Lord is
upon you, and a deep darkness is on the people. (Isaiah 60 NKJV)

God is summoning His warrior daughters to arise, to 'get out of
bed.' He is calling you. He has a plan for you. He is shining the light
of His glory over you, to influence and lead. He wants to use your
stories of salvation, redemption, wanderings, escapades, and
revelation to touch people. He wants you to rise up in the glory
& story of all He is, in and through you, in your own perfectly
imperfect way!

Throughout scripture we see God choosing, calling, and anointing individuals. To do a work, fulfill a purpose, to be the difference in some seemingly random situation. But there is nothing random about who He has made you and is making you to be. You are a leader and He intends to use you if you're willing. Our focus must consistently be: to rise up in the better story He is calling us to, no matter what it looks like in the natural.

God asked me to sit for seven years on the mountain top with Him. I like to say Jesus home-schooled me. I did little else in that time but study His Word. To my flesh, in the natural, it was torture at times. I was like a racehorse stuck in the starting gate, bucking to get out, to run hard and fast. I wanted to get to work, to do this "calling thing" big, and my way. But every effort was thwarted until I settled into Him to work on myself.

I had to keep letting Him teach and break me. All I knew was He was good, I trusted Him, and I wanted more of Him. We peeled back layer after layer of old wounds and healed them. We wrestled for control again and again - I didn't win. I often envisioned a Rocky movie when Rocky is just getting the snot knocked out of him. He's pummeled and bloody laying on the matt and you wish he would win. But you want desperately to yell out, "Just stay down, please just stay down!" Well, I finally learned to 'stay down,' and how to love better, stronger, and more freely because of it.

My personal life was turned upside down because of this 'wrestling match,' this new story God had for me. My marriage almost didn't survive it. My children and some of my friends pushed me away. Life was in an upheaval on every front. But I clung to Jesus and His better story. Not only did He prove faithful. He taught me a new strength, confidence, and freedom, that couldn't come from my own exhaustible will. But only His undying, unchanging, perfect love.

I am not a scholarly writer, I haven't made a name for myself doing anything in particular. I just keep "getting out of bed" in response to His call. 'Getting up' everyday to meet Him where He will lead me next. I'm getting less stubborn. Learning to just say,"Yes, Lord" a lot quicker. And I'm in love, once again, with the adventure of a new chapter in my story. "Getting out of bed," or "showing up," is all He is asking you to do as well.

I hope you are excited about the next chapter in your story too. Will you rise and meet Him in it? How will He use it to touch hearts, break molds, make noise, fuel faith, and affect change?

I pray God will liberate you spiritually, encourage you personally, and guide you to lead, in the unique and individual love story, He is authoring through you! Because that is how, from this vantage point in history, and in His story, we will be effective.

The world desperately needs to see, hear, and feel your divine story and bright light.

To lead or not to lead, that is not the question...

By default, if you are following Christ, you are leading. The question is how will you be effective at it, at this point, in Kingdom history?

Well, when Shakespeare authored "to be or not to be," he was establishing for Hamlet, whether or not to exist. When the apostle Paul pondered his existence, he concluded that to die was gain, but to live is Christ.

So since we do exist, we follow Christ, and to live is Christ. If this is true, then we are to be, work, and lead as Christ, the light of the world. However He may be fashioning that in us as individuals.

"Everything rises and falls on leadership."

- John Maxwell

I have always loved this quote by John Maxwell and I wholeheartedly agree with him. But I believe there is a thinking or stereotype that exists in the word "leader," that makes people instantly disqualify themselves (in their minds). So the word leader is worth defusing and defining clearly before we move on.

The dictionary (dictionary.com) defines the word leader as: A person who rules, guides or inspires others. To which I also agree, but leads us to the next question: What inspires or moves a person to rule, guide, and inspire others?

I believe it is God, love, and what we have learned in this life about both, that cause us to rise up, move, and take action. By default this is leading. Which brings us to my handy dandy acronym for the word lead: It is to be a:

Living
Example of
All God has
Done or is Doing - In your life. It's truly that simple.

Whatever 'it' is for you, whatever you're living or your story has taught you thus far. It is time to rise up in it, share, and lead by example. You are just like the sun cresting the horizon on a fresh summer morning. Bringing hope, nurture, and possibility with your story and example. In so doing, just as the sun rising in the noonday sky intensifies, so will you in your effectiveness, as a warrior of light, aka leader.

What Kind Of Leader Are You?

See if you recognize yourself in any of these four descriptions.

"The Wind Beneath Their Wings" Leader

You are the encourager, the one who lifts others up. You see and hear potential in others, and live to cultivate it. Helping them become more effective in their personal calling. Please take this in: You are absolutely vital to the growth and success of others. Without you, there would be anguished weeping in heaven over a lot of lost potential.

Recently, I read a blog post by a respected pastor. In it, the pastor asks if you can answer a few questions about who some people were in history. For example: Who visited with Dwight L. Moody in a shoe store and spoke to him about Christ? Who were the parents of the godly and gifted Daniel?

If you are like me, I vividly remember the stories, but not the names of those people who were the support system and/or catalyst for the famous persons growth. But this pastor encourages us not to dismiss lightly the idea that we cannot remember their names. Because without them our church history, and therefore our today, would look very different.

It is important to note,1 Corinthians 12, says, "Some of the parts that seem the most weak or unimportant, are the most necessary." Never discount your leadership in the form of being the wind beneath another's wings. God uses you to help others take flight, and in His beautifully harmonious way, it causes you to soar too!

At the end of your personal story on earth, you will look at life's stage, and see all of those you encouraged and cultivated. You will be able to draw your curtain in peace and joyful fulfillment, leaving behind a legacy of hearts, stories, and leaders, full of Jesus.

Because you took the time, love, and energy to walk with them and lift them up.

I cannot over-emphasize the value and importance of this role, particularly in these current times.

Helpful Hint: Make sure you are filling your lamp daily with Jesus. You cannot give what you do not have. Recognize your own needs, that you do indeed have them, and care for yourself as needed. As natural born givers, it is easy to become depleted. Do something that makes you feel lighthearted and even silly. Worship in the form of dance, singing, or walk and pray. It will give you the fuel you need to be the blessing that you are.

Exercise: Listen to the song "Wind Beneath My Wings," By Bette Midler. Really, download and listen to it. Imagine all of those grateful lifted hearts and lives you have encouraged, singing this to you. When you are done ask yourself these questions: How does it make you feel? What will you do with that feeling? Write a prayer or psalm to God about it.

"The Bringing The Heat" Leader

Most of us who are called to lead in some way really like the idea of being in front, in the abstract. It is fun to think of being a face or name known for change and trailblazing. The one recognized as the "go to" or "expert" for a niche or topic. And I believe there is truth in that thinking, as it has a lot of very fun aspects.

But if this is you, if you are the face standing in front, you have a load to carry, and we need you. You are brave, strong, and willing, you are doing one of the hardest jobs on the planet, being first and in front. While we are all chosen to represent, and be ambassadors for Christ. You are called to do it in a very visible way. It opens you up to scrutiny, attack, and to be inundated with people wanting you and your time. We need you to be the example of how to do this well, not perfect, but as your best example of Jesus. Our world is in desperate need of Christ-centered leaders, you are it, and out in front.

You will deal with loneliness. Trying to find where or if you fit in places and often you won't. You'll be misunderstood and uncertain a lot of the time. It's okay, it is just part of the job description and why God makes you strong and brave.

For you, serving the message (or the work), is more important than the stuff that shows up to stop you. Please hear all of these as positives and part of the job. Each of these things I have listed are the things that keep you growing and out in front. They help you become a good navigator, able to steer around, go over, and through whatever shows up in your path.

Like Jesus, your identity must be rooted in God the Father, and your mindset one of possibility, authority, redemption, grace, and love. Be real, be human, and publicly show us how you love Him with your whole heart, soul, mind, and strength, and others will listen and follow.

There are many great examples and even other definitions and stories of leadership that would be worthy of sharing, as examples. But in the interest of simplifying an often overcomplicated topic, let's just stick to Jesus. He is leadership personified, period. He knew His identity and mission in God. He set His face toward Jerusalem, did not look left or right, and went about doing His Father's business all along the way. That is the only example those leading in front need.

Your sights are set on glory, with the goal of one day hearing, "Well done good and faithful servant." Your business along the way is standing up, speaking and pouring out, sacrifice, and fully expressed love.

Helpful Hint:
Surround yourself with an inner circle of trust worthy and supportive individuals: the encouragers, the wise counsel, the accountability people. Those that will challenge you in love. Jesus had His twelve, and even narrowed those to sometimes three, two, or one to be with Him for certain moments and events. Just like Jesus, your inner circle is vital to doing your work.

Leading, being the example, and making disciples at the same time is a big job. I am taking for granted that you pray, get in the Word everyday, and talk to and listen for God...all day everyday. But that bears saying, for apart from Him we can literally do nothing.

Exercise: Your Board of Trustees
Think of at least two people you can ask, reach out to, or spend time with that can be one of your 'inner circle' people. Decide,

how you will have time with these people, as you need them, going forward.

You also need a person, or people, who are out in front of you a bit, for directional purposes. Recently, I attended the Storyline Conference at Willow Creek. It was amazing. At the conference, I believe it was Donald Miller who said, that having what he calls "horizon people," is good for direction. A horizon person is someone who is 'out in front' of you, just in the distance, and where you would like to be.

Pick one or two horizon people, leaders of light, who are doing the things that you want to be doing. Maybe share this with your inner circle so they can support you in that direction. Who is God making you into as a leader of light? How can you better embody that identity now? Here is a suggestion: just start saying out loud and often, "I am a (whatever He is making you next or more of)_____. (i.e. teacher, writer, singer, preacher, artist, parent, more loving, sacrificial, patient). Take some time with this, pray about it, ask God for revelation, remember: His pace is peace.

Then declare it regularly and with authority, in private and in public. You will be amazed at how much more effectively you will step into and become it.

Write a prayer thanking God for all the ways He has taught and grown you as a leader thus far. Then let Him know you are ready for whatever He wants to do in, to, and through you now. A 'comfort zone' is a sneaky form of oppression, that keeps you stuck and settling. So, I triple dog dare you, to ask God and lead.

_____

_____

_____

_____

_____

_____

_____

_____

_____

_____

_____

_____

_____

"The Soft Clouds Of Comfort Leader"

In sickness, adversity, and in death God is our constant comfort. One of the glorious ways He comforts us, is how He uses you and your heart of compassion and mercy, to comfort those you see in need.

You are the leader who's heart is like a soft and billowing cloud that envelopes and loves on us. You see the ones who need a ride to church, an ear to listen and understand, a heart-space for our messiness to be okay. You keep showing up to do the behind-the-scenes ministry of constant caring, in many shapes and forms.

You are usually quiet and unassuming with great faith and trust in the Lord. You are a rock of grace and peace to all who need you. We turn to you when we are broken, hurting, and even desperate. You are God's gentle and loving arms that embrace us and whisper words of love and encouragement.

This lost and hurting world needs you, but I believe other lost and hurting Christians need you even more right now. The ones who are disgruntled, who have wandered, who are growing and confused. They need your compassion, grace, and Jesus-filled heart that beckons, "It's okay, you're okay, come to me, I love you with an unfailing love."

The mercy and compassion you lead with makes it possible and okay for us to walk into Jesus' arms, and find hope, healing, peace, and possibility, that maybe, just maybe, everything will be okay. You are a trusted and needed leader in a world full of heart-ache and discouragement.

You rarely allow yourself to complain or speak a negative word about another person. But finding a space to comfort your own soul and ways to put oil in your own lamp, is vital to maintaining your energy and capacity to give so well.

Helpful Hint:
Think of at least two people and/or activities that fill you up and bring you joy. Write them here:

_____

_____

_____

Write these people/activities into your calendar this month, and every month for the remainder of the year. Make it a regular habit to cultivate joy, laughter, and well-being for yourself. Then you will be full and ready to overflow with the healing love and compassion of Jesus.

<u>"The Rainbow Leader"</u>

These leaders are the colorful moms, sisters, aunts, cousins, grandmothers, and girlfriends that bring an overarching and foundational peace, stability, and practicality, that society and sanity require.

If this is you rejoice! For while you may sometimes feel unappreciated, neglected, and wanting to be seen and heard more, without you we would go stark raving mad. Seriously, I am convinced if we did not have those strong women of grounded-ness and nurture, we would lose our minds. You come with the ability to ask poignant questions like, "What on earth are you thinking?" "Do you really think it's a good idea to sell everything and move there?" or "Is that relationship really healthy for you?" And an all time favorite of mine, the plain and direct, "Really?"

These are the strong and authentic souls that lead and support from alongside of us, all while wiping noses, making meals, and doing the ministry work of availability and truth-telling. They listen to our whiny crap and secretly want to smack us into reality, but reply instead with a practical comment that is helpful and honest. I love these women so much, because I truly need them.

This type of leadership is emotional work, and if this is you, please never underestimate the power and necessity of your leadership. Both for the next generation, and for those of us who sometimes feel we are caught in a whirlwind. When we see you at our side, we take a breath, and know everything is going to be okay, just because you are there. You are a beacon of light and sanity, in a world of chaos and "e"-everything. You remind us of simplicity, family, dinner time, swing-sets, and macaroni and cheese, when everything around us says, "Go faster."

I refer to you as rainbow leaders, because emotionally and sometimes physically. You cover the color spectrum in the hats and faces you must wear to serve and lead those that need your beautiful light.

<u>Helpful Hint:</u>
Find a task, project, or group that gives you a sense of meaning and contribution. Short-term goals and achievements that use more of your intellect, giving you a break from all of your emotional work.

Make a list of a few things that are currently in your awareness that you might find interesting to join, volunteer at, or even start:

_____

_____

_____

_____
_____
_____
_____
_____

Write a prayer thanking God for the strong emotional gifts and abilities He has blessed you with. Ask Him if or what He would like you to contribute to next.

_____
_____
_____
_____
_____
_____
_____

Remember, "Everything rises and falls on leadership." It makes no difference what station in life you stand in. You are a leader. You are the answer in this messy world. Rise.

Let There Be Light

And God said, "Let there be light," and there was light. God saw
the light was good; and He separated the light from the darkness."
- Genesis 1:3-4 (NIV)

Notice, when God said, "Let there be light," the sun started
shining. He told it to do something and it just did it. It didn't say,
"Oh, what if people don't really want me to shine? What if my
rays aren't good enough? Or why bother, no one will care if I do?"
It simply burst forth in its bold, brilliant calling and purpose to
radiate warmth and presence. To nurture and grow all things
under and around it, and be light in the darkness, attracting
and drawing life to it. You are the light, the difference in the
darkness.

As a woman called by God, this is how you are being asked to
light up and lead right where you are. To take your identity,
calling, and story from God and without doubt or hesitation start
shining in it. Just because He told you to. It is the only reason or
permission you will ever need.

This is how I believe He is asking us to lead; throwing off
weights, sins, darkness, earthly cares, and temporal things to
be light, just because He told us to. Putting on Christ as light,
that we might shine so before men. That they would see our

good works and glorify our Father in Heaven, and that many lives might be saved.

Let's look at another example of responding to God's call while Jesus, the Light of the world, was on earth. When Jesus began the work of calling disciples, He walked along the banks of the water where he saw Simon Peter, James, and Andrew and Jesus simply said, "Follow me," and they immediately did. They got out of the boat, no questions, no roadmap, outcome unknown, and followed. They had no idea where they were going or what would become of them. They were leaving all they and their ancestors had ever known or done, and just followed. They ignored all cultural and familial security in response and obedience to Jesus saying, "Come, follow me, I will make you fishers of men."

So powerful are those words; "Come, follow me." We don't follow by accident, we choose to follow because our heart is in it. What is on your heart today? What is keeping you from jumping out of your boat to keep pace with the One who promises, "I will make you become fishers of men?" (Matthew 4:19)

Take a moment to think about how far God has brought you and all that you have overcome in Him. He still bids you, "Come, follow me." He is inviting you to a wondrous life and adventure in Him, found in abandon obedience.

"Be strong and courageous. Do not be afraid or terrified because of them, for the Lord your God goes with you; He will never leave you nor forsake you."

- Deuteronomy 31:6 (NIV)

"For my yoke is easy and my burden is light."

- Matthew 11:30 (NIV)

What is hindering you from keeping pace with Jesus, in where is leading you, in your life?

_____
_____
_____
_____
_____
_____
_____
_____

Are you ready to lovingly give it to God? Remember that where the spirit of the Lord is there is freedom.

_____
_____
_____
_____
_____
_____
_____
_____
_____
_____

Write a prayer, poem, song, or just journal about possibility, in all that you believe Jesus has for you to become and do:

(You may want a separate piece of writing paper.)

_____

_____

_____

_____

_____

_____

_____

_____

_____

_____

_____

_____

_____

_____

It is no coincidence that you dream what you dream, as being possible. God authors us, our stories, and our hearts desire.

Take a joyful and simple step in the direction of your possibility, just because He told you to. Remember, it is the only reason or permission you ever need. And Let there be YOUR light.

Called

"Before I formed you in your mother's womb I chose you. Before you were born I set you apart. I appointed you to be a prophet to the nations."

- Jeremiah 1:5 (NET)

Going first in anything sounds good in the abstract. We want to be trail blazers and world changers for God. But the truth is to go first you take risks. You risk that someone will walk away. That maybe you will no longer belong in that group, that church, or that business. Most importantly, you risk your heart, because being light, being God's expression or art work in the world, is scary stuff.

This means you have to walk fully surrendered, allowing and being willing for Him to express His spirit through you. Bringing the heat, radiance, and color that only you can bring.

Let's look at how Jeremiah reacted when God called him to speak and do something, something that wasn't exactly popular I might add.

But I love Jeremiah's response when God called him to go and speak to people:

Then said I: "Ah, Lord God! Behold I cannot speak, for I am a youth."

- Jeremiah 1:6 (NKJV)

God is calling him, and he is already denying his ability, experience, and readiness. I say I love it, because I can relate to it. Maybe you can too.

When we are called by God to step up it is not a light or easy thing. But it is a privilege, the Creator is speaking to you. Like Jeremiah we can forget one irrefutable fact, we are His. Before we were even matter in our mother's womb He knew us. He set us apart. He chose and authored us into this current scene, to lead. Yet we tend to stare Him in the face and hesitate, question, deny, and wrestle with the thing He is asking us to do next. Believe me, God and I have been to the wrestling mats many times, and I'm happy to report He wins, every time.

What is God asking you to do next? (No thinking, just knee-jerk from your spirit.)

_____

_____

_____

_____

_____

_____

_____

_____

_____

_____

_____

_____

Let's see how God replies to Jeremiah; please read Jeremiah 1:7-10 (NKJV).

7 But the Lord said to me:
Do not say, 'I am a youth,'
For you shall go to all to whom I send you,
And whatever I command you, you shall Speak.
8 Do not be afraid of their faces,
For I am with you to deliver you, says the Lord.
9 Then the Lord put forth His hand and touched my mouth, and the Lord said to me:
Behold, I have put My words in your mouth.
10 See, I have this day set you over the nations and over the kingdoms,
To root out and to pull down,
To destroy and to throw down,
To build and to plant.

I have to say that God's sovereignty and authority utterly humbles and thrills me all at the same time. How about you?

God replies to Jeremiah, "Do not say, I am a youth." He is not going to accept Jeremiah's estimation of himself, or focus on the natural.

God tells him he will go to whom? _____

And speak what?_____

There was nothing for Jeremiah to do except listen and obey, God was going to do the work. Jeremiah only needed to be willing and courageous. Why courageous? Look at verse 8, what does God know Jeremiah is feeling in order to tell him, "Don't be afraid of their faces?"_____

_____
_____

Fear. Fear is the most common emotion when we are told "don't be afraid" What does God know we must have a fear of to add, "of their faces?"

_____
_____
_____
_____
_____
_____
_____

Whenever we are called to speak anything to people, to take a stand or make a declaration, or even share in a group, there can be fear. Isn't it fear of rejection, judgement, or failure, in front of people that keeps us lip-locked and frozen?

How does God answer that in the second part of verse 8?

_____

_____

_____

_____

_____

_____

_____

_____

God is never going to call you to something He hasn't already gone before you to prepare, or isn't going to go through with you. He walks right along side you, holding your right hand. It is His work after all and He will deliver you from their faces, whatever expressions they may hold. Our job is to say, "Yes, Lord" and take another step in wholehearted faith that He has written the script, He knows the lines, the ending, and the outcome. Victory!

You are called, onward Christian soldier!

Pick A Fight

"When one rules justly over men, ruling in the fear of God, He dawns on them like the morning light, like the sun shining forth on a cloudless morning, like rain that makes grass to sprout from the earth."

                                                            - 2 Samuel 23:3-4 (ESV)

In David's last words written in 2 Samuel 23 (ESV) above, the King and sweet psalmist of Israel shares that: "The spirit of the Lord spoke by me, and His word was on my tongue." When he describes how those who rule must be: "Like the light of the morning when the sun rises." Sounds like bringing hope to me, and in order to bring hope, we must rise up.

What will love cause you to rise up in and do?

There is something in your soul that causes you to rise up. Something that when confronted with it, you want to make a difference. A place inside you where your spirit feels like it will swell into your throat and burst out of your mouth, and you can barely contain it. Usually, it is some form or blend of justice, freedom, love, hope, or passionate expression.

What lights you up or ticks you off? What is it that has you saying to yourself, 'I can do something better about that thing I see happening?'

I have always been deeply passionate about people's life stories and how and why they live them the way they do. I wonder what causes people to love boldly enough to take a stand. Even if it means risking their reputation, safety, or lives.

I watched my grandma live her life story. I spent a lot of time at her house, to escape the chaos at mine. In reality, I was just exchanging it for a different version of chaos and dysfunction. I loved her so much and she hated her life. But she didn't have anyone else's house to go to. So she would escape her life, by hiding at the bottom of a whiskey bottle.

She suffered physical and emotional abuse and drank to stay sane and alive. But whiskey bottles became prison bars that kept her self-imprisoned and miserable.

One night when I was about ten or eleven years old I was spending the night at her house. I would sit on the living room floor and watch tv. My grandpa watched in the bedroom after years of the same scenario playing out. Grandma would start to drink and she would be laughing and talking and then out of no where she would go quiet. This is what I came to refer to as, "The eye of the storm." When the eye of the storm came this was the time, your cue to vacate the room. Because after the "eye" anyone within sight was targeted for a massive verbal assault.

Well, I was watching the Love Boat, and I love stories. I had to know what was going to happen to these people's lives. Now that they were wrapping up their time on the boat with Doc, Julie, and Isaac. That's when the eye of the storm came. But I didn't care, I wasn't budging, I had to know the end of these people's stories!

The verbal attack began. I heard about all the ways that I was a burden to her and how my siblings and I were ruining her life. She began to list all the negativities she could think of about me, and ended her sentence with, "And you have a ___ big mouth, that's your problem!"

Before I even knew what I was doing something rose up in me and I sprang to my feet. I went into the kitchen grabbed her whiskey bottle, stomped back into the living room, set it on top of the tv and said, "Yeah, well there's your problem!"

Suddenly she went quiet, and my eyes went like saucers, I thought, 'Oh crap she is going to kill me.' I spun on my heels and made a mad dash for the bedroom and shut the door. She bellowed down the hallway for my grandpa to come and beat me for disrespecting her. Thankfully, he must have already fallen asleep.

I laid in my bed that night and cried quietly. Not out of fear but out of anger and a broken heart. I was angry that my grandma wouldn't fight for her own life. I saw her beautiful heart, every time she showed up when I called her at some ungodly hour of the day or night, to save me from my life. I had heard her laughter many times before, right from her heart and soul, filled with joy, and I wanted that grandma. I wanted her to fight for her life, her freedom, her joy, and I didn't care about my safety in that moment. I didn't care if my grandpa beat me. I wanted to stand up and speak the truth. To call out the lie of all the hiding, dysfunction, and abuse in defense of her life and mine. And yes, I still wanted to hear how the stories on the Love Boat ended!

What truth do you need to take a stand for in your life? Our world needs women who will stand up for the truth, in all the lies and chaos, whatever the risk, for love.

Who do you love enough, to risk even your safety, for a better world and story? I can't help but think of Esther when she said, "If I perish, I perish." (Esther 4:16 NASB) She spoke those words out of love for her family and her people. For a generation that would come after her. She risked it all in faith and love. The kind of burning love that takes a risk in the scary things for the hope of a better thing.

Esther's faith in God and love for her people allowed her to be victorious. My grandma's love for her grand-daughter ultimately allowed her to be victorious too. Later, when I was about 15 years old and I was living with my friend, I got sick. I'll spare you the details but suffice it to say I couldn't sip water without it going immediately through me. This had gone on for days and I was weak and dehydrated, and now there was lots of blood.

I called her late in the evening to ask her if she could please take me to the emergency room. But she had already hit the bottom of the whiskey bottle. She told me to pack a bag and she would come and get me as she had always done. I asked her to put my grandpa on the phone. I told him I was going to find a ride to the emergency room and if they called for permission to treat me (because I was a minor) would he please just say yes, he agreed.

I was admitted to the hospital. I was alone and really scared, thinking the worst. The nurse came in telling me I had a call on the line. I picked up the phone and it was my mother. My heart leapt in hope of some nurture and reassurance, I needed a mother right then.

But she was in jail and looking for a way out. She tried desperately to convince me I had cancer and was dying, so the guards or whomever was listening might have pity on her and let her out, to supposedly come and see me. With a sigh of familiarity of her ways, my heart sank, and I hung up and started to cry.

Just then, my grandpa walked in my room. I asked, "What are you doing here?"

He said, "Well I have to be up here now because your grandma checked herself into the ART center this morning."

After many intervention meetings and counseling sessions, I knew ART stood for Alcohol Rehab Treatment center.

I was in shock, I snapped my head up, "What?" I said, "Grandma is in rehab?"

"Yeah," he replied with some disgust in his voice. "After she realized you called last night and she was too drunk to help you, she checked herself in this morning."

I couldn't believe my ears. I was stunned and skeptical but my heart swelled with hope.

The nurse wheeled my grandma in right at that moment, and there she was, in a wheel chair, in rehab, and she spoke the words herself. She said, "I checked myself into the ART center today, and I am sorry I couldn't take you to the hospital last night."

Alcoholics are difficult to believe, but I believed her. I believed she wanted to be well. She never drank after that to my knowledge.

She struggled with other addictions and issues, but she didn't drink. I chalk that up to a huge victory for love and the power of it. She took a stand in love over alcohol and won. Love wins, every time, even if we don't get to see the "win" in the moment. Taking a stand for love always, always, wins! So I encourage you to believe that, and take a stand for love in your life and for this world He came to save, as we engage one heart and story at a time. There is something, someone, worth risking your heart, safety, addictions, ego, idols, and insecurities for...take your stand in love, with love and for love.

What causes you to stand up? An injustice? An oppression? A need? A holy discontent in your soul? Write about it here:

_____

_____

_____

_____

_____

_____

_____

_____

_____

_____

_____

_____

_____

_____

How could you lead with love in it?

_____

_____

_____

_____

_____

_____

_____

_____

_____

_____

_____

_____

Write a prayer asking for God's love and guidance in your next step:

_____

_____

_____

_____

_____

_____

_____

_____

_____

_____

What do you think God is saying your next steps could be?

_____

_____

_____

_____

_____

_____

_____

_____

_____

How will you respond to what you have discovered?

_____

_____

_____

_____

_____

_____

_____

_____

_____

_____

_____

Set To Rule

God knew you, knows you, created you, and wrote your beautiful story before you were even matter in your mother's womb. I find that breath-taking. He had an original role and intention for you before the foundations of the earth, within His epic love story called "Life." That role and intention was leadership.

But isn't it funny how often we don't move forward in our story and callings because we wait for permission. Like someone's going to walk up to us one day and say, "You can now go ahead and live the thing you know God has put you on the planet to do." I know I did. In my insecurities I was afraid to get it wrong, mess it up, or offend someone. So I just waited, or half-heartedly tried, to see what would happen.

No one is coming to give us permission except God. And It is our job to respond in obedience when He does. Not waiting in insecurity for in reality that is sin.

I just had lunch with my good friend Carol she is a light and joy in my life. We were discussing predestination, being chosen, free will and grace, light-hearted lunch stuff. But regardless of where you stand on all of that, if you are a saved person, at some point God chose you. Because no one comes to Jesus unless the father firsts draws him. (John 6:44 NIV)

Just the humility, the privilege, and responsibility, of being a chosen of God in any fashion ought to bring us to quick response of obedience. We get to be the light, the hands, the feet, the bringers of the presence of Jesus to a world that desperately needs Him. This in my mind, puts waiting for the permission of another human being, to act on what we know God is calling us to, into the category of absurdity.

For clarification I am not talking about self-righteousness, or running off willy nilly on a whim of emotion we think, 'could be' from God. I am talking about a point of revelation where you know, that you know, what He is telling you.

But just in case you doubt your authority as the light in the world, I found some scripture to help us see the truth of our being set to rule as such. And the only reason we ever need to do so is: He said so.

"And God made two great lights; the greater light to rule the day, and the lesser light to rule the night: he made the stars also. And God set them in the firmament of the heaven to give light on the earth, and to rule over the day and over the night, and to divide the light from the darkness"

- Genesis 1:16-18 (AKJV)

God is always setting and using light to rule and guide in some fashion. He uses us as light in varying capacities, based on our faith, to rule as well.

Those who are wise shall shine like the brightness of the firmament, and those who turn many to righteousness like the stars forever and ever.

- Daniel 12:3 (NKJV)

The commentary on this verse in Daniel (by John MacArthur) says: To shine in glory is a privilege of all the saved (along with the principle of 1 Thess. 2:12; 1Peter 5:10 NKJV) Any who influence others for righteousness shine like stars in varying capacities of light as their reward (as in 1 Corinthians 3:8 NKJV). The faithfulness of the believer's witness will determine one's eternal capacity to reflect God's glory.

"For the Lord God is a sun and shield; The Lord will give grace and glory; no good thing will He withhold From those who walk uprightly."

- Psalm 84:11 (ERV)

Our Lord Jesus is referred to as a sun, a light sent to rule by day and by night.

We see again and again throughout scripture how God uses light to lead, to guide, and for signs and wonders on the earth. Light is established authority on the earth, and the Light of the world lives in you as an authority as well. You are a ruler of light, a sign, and a wonder to the Gentiles, because of the Light and authority that lives in you.

We have the privilege, authority, and the responsibility to live and lead like it. By doing so, we hold back the darkness. We are chosen, adopted, heirs, and the reigning, governing, authority on this earth.

In the first chapter of Genesis, immediately following God establishing the earth and all living things on it, He establishes dominion:

Then God said, "Let us make mankind in our image, in our likeness, so that they may rule over the fish in the sea and the birds in the sky, over the livestock and all the wild animals, and over all the creatures that move along the ground."

> - Genesis 1:26 (NIV)

Then God blessed them, and God said to them, "Be fruitful and multiply. Fill the earth and govern it. Reign over the fish in the sea, the birds in the sky, and all the animals that scurry along the ground."

> - Genesis 1:28 (NLT)

You are a light, a sign, a wonder, a guide, a masterpiece, a leader. Reign on this earth, by letting God's powerful, colorful, radiant love and light shine through you!

Do not question, hold back, or deny who He is in you, and how He wants to rule and reign through you. Jesus came at very dark time to save the world, He is still saving it. Through His powerful remnant of light on the earth: you and the church body as a whole. We, as His holy people, His chosen, His church, are set to rule on this earth.

"But the path of the just is as the shining light, that shines more and more to the perfect day."

- Proverbs 4:18 (AKJV)

Let Go - Free Yourself First

"Old things have passed away, your love has stayed the same, your constant grace remains the cornerstone." - "Jesus We Love You" - Bethel Music & Paul McClure.

You cannot lead anyone or anything else, if you cannot first lead yourself. The first step in freeing and leading yourself well, is to let go of the past. It may not be quick or easy but surrender all of it to God, and let Him work through it, with you. You must lay it at His feet, ask Him to heal you, teach you, and redeem those things that hurt you, that He might use them for good.

Throughout the process of writing this book I found myself stopping again and again, I just knew there was some old stuff attached to it. I really hate that when it happens. Because I would like to think that if we address an issue in our lives, we should be able to just move on, and it should be behind us. Right? Wrong.

When it happens I'm almost offended, like 'how dare this one thing keep showing up and getting in my way!' Then I realize I can get mad at it or go to God with it. Like a stubborn, cranky, toddler I go to my Father and ask, "What do I do with this? And why do I keep stopping?"

And as God and luck would have it, wouldn't you know He shows up and answers me. Immediately I'm thinking, 'Here we go again with that stupid vulnerability thing...He is going to make me emotionally go through something with Him.' The idea is exhausting, but I trust Him more than myself, so I say, "Ok Lord, let's do this. Please show me what's stopping me."

For days after asking God, I keep flashing on a scene in my life, where I am standing outside Tampa International Airport, watching my dad drive away. I'm about 13 years old, and in one of my many attempts to escape life with my mother, I asked my dad if I could come and live with him. He flew to Michigan to get me, and I will never forget how happy I was as we boarded the plane to fly back to Florida together. Just as we were about to step from the gangway onto the plane he put his arm around my shoulders and gave me a squeeze that felt like love and pride.

My dad was an alcoholic and a gentle spirit. I always felt he didn't have the capacity to handle very much, almost frail. Most evenings he was drunk by dinner time, and toward the end of the meal, my half-siblings would run off to play. I would sit at the table with him more hungry for his love and attention, than the food on the table.

Then he would start to cry. My heart would break because I loved him and at the same time, I would sear with anger, that I was in the position to be caring for him. Through his tears he would confess his inability and guilt for not being a good father, and I would reassure him that he was.

I wanted to turn that table over and scream, you coward! Stand up, act like a man, a father, and a husband. How dare you burden those you love with your cowardliness! But I sat seething and reassuring him he was a good father to me. I hated that lie, and I hated the foreigner I felt like in his home. Not to mention, attending a new high school was torture at that age. So, after a few months, I wanted to go back to Michigan.

When I told my dad I wanted to go back to Michigan, he went silent. He looked furious. I had no idea how he would react. I hadn't lived with him long enough to know how he dealt with anger. He told me to pack my things. The family loaded into the car a couple days later and we drove to Tampa International.

He pulled up out front, still not speaking a word to me. He went inside and my heart was pounding out of my chest. No one in the car was saying a word either. The tension felt like the moment when you wonder if someone is about to hit you. He came out and took my bag out of the trunk and set it on the curb. He opened my car door, handed me a ticket, and I got out. He got back in the car and drove away.

I stood there in disbelief. My mind was reeling and I was trying to fathom that he just left me there. The questions began: What do I do? Where do I go? Did he really just leave me here? Then panic started to creep in. I am a girl, alone. What if someone tries to kidnap me, or hurt me? What am I going to do?

Hurt, devastation, panic, fear, and loneliness gripped me, tears started to well in my eyes. I swallowed hard and pushed back the emotion. In spite and determination, I picked up my bag and walked into the airport.

I walked up to the giant black board with changing cities and times on it, knowing I had to look for Detroit and the time that was on my ticket, to find my gate. I was so scared someone would discover I was alone. I took on a very stoic demeanor in an attempt to appear confident, as I stood there gazing at the board.

I finally saw what I believed to be the correct gate number and began to follow the signs to its location. I suddenly realized I was going to have to get on one of those little tram cars to ride to a different section of the airport, and I was terrified to get it wrong. I followed the signs and the crowd trying to blend in. I got on the tram and literally sat on the edge of the seat.

I felt like every eye was on me, everyone knew I was alone, and I was vulnerable. When the doors opened I shot out of that tram and continued to follow the signs to the gate. At this point I was fighting tears of fear. What if I am on the wrong plane? What if my mother doesn't show up to get me when I get there? What if someone hurts me before I can make it back?

I took my seat and it felt like a hug as I nestled into it and started to buckle my seat belt. I was hanging on every syllable when the captain came over the speaker to make announcements. He told the approximate flight time and then the weather and arrival time, "Into Detroit." I heard the word Detroit, and a wave of relief and peace came over me and I sank further into my seat. For a moment I could enjoy the sun streaming in through the small window across my lap, and the free glass of soda on my tray. My mother and grandmother showed up to get me.

When I asked God to show me what was stopping me now, and I kept flashing to standing there watching the tail lights of my dads car as he drove away. The scene seemed to pan backwards a bit, and there stood Jesus, with His hands on my shoulders. "Your earthly father drove away that day, but I have always had you in my hands. I walked with you through that airport, onto that tram and airplane, you were never alone," He said to me. Then I got a picture of what seemed to be legions of angels literally engulfing both sides of me, as I had walked through that airport. (A vision that has brought tremendous healing, peace, and understanding.)

That experience with my dad taught me that I was easily disposable. That if I did something 'wrong' I could be not just dismissed. But even put in harms way, from someone I thought loved me. God revealed to me how I was putting those same thoughts and ideas on Him. Believing that if the work, the book, the anything I might try and do for Him wasn't good enough, He would leave me. Intellectually, I knew better, but our old stuff can show up to get into our new stuff and we have to go to Him with it, sometimes again and again. Which as I said earlier, I really hate, so I asked God to heal and deliver me from that story. He did one better. He healed me, delivered me, and showed me the redemptive perspective.

My dad wasn't angry at me, he was angry at himself. I was only the living affirmation in my leaving, that his fears were true, he indeed was not the father he knew he could be. Light is like that. When God uses someone as light, it exposes darkness, and the person being light is reacted at, in all sorts of ways.

I wondered, what didn't he get as a youth, that left him so drunk, so inept, so broken, and unable to love well? By all worldly standards he was a good and hard working man with a big heart. Who or what did this to him? I seem to naturally arrive at a story analogy.

In any good story or screenplay, the first thing that is determined in developing the main character is: what do they want? The individual or character needs or wants something that drives them to take action.

In our human stories, we are born and before we even know how to form a thought, the thing we desperately both need and want is unconditional love. It is in our DNA to need and want it, because unconditional love, is God. God is unconditional love and He designed us to seek and find Him for it, for ourselves.

Next in a storyline, after we learn some personal quirks and niceties about the character, comes the resistance. The thing that challenges or stands in the way of what the main character wants and/or needs. In life-story terms, this is where the world enters into the plot. The world, with its messed up humans, darkness and ideas about what love is, and feels like, in every possible form of distraction from the real thing.

Then the main character must choose, either the thinking, ideas, and pursuit of the world, that only provides short-term fixes of love in counterfeit, or, the One that is love personified. (Laying down the belief that unconditional love can ever come from anything in this world. In exchange for a love so unconditional and powerful it fills you until you overflow.) It frees you from worldly ideas of love, and the blind oppression it causes. It makes your insides feel mounted on eagles wings, to soar above the noise and clamor, to bask in radiant, electric love.

We're TOLD we want money, we want unconditional love.
We're TOLD we want acceptance, we want unconditional love.
We're TOLD we want more and bigger stuff, we want unconditional love.
We're TOLD we want titles, admiration, and fame, we want unconditional love.

I'm not exactly sure what happened in my dad's early life story, and how or why he didn't find God's unconditional love. I wished he had. But thankfully God taught me how to forgive and unconditionally love my dad, as time brought healing.

It also brought him sobriety, and a long hard battle with throat cancer. Interestingly, my sister and I talked about how sad it was that he could not orally express love well, and the cancer showed up first in his mouth, then his throat.

He loved the outdoors. He had built a home for he and my step-mom, (who is a pillar of strength), on the side of a mountain in southern Oregon. When she called me to say that if I wanted any more time with him, I had better come, I went. I had so many emotions, including desperation to get to him, to just let him know that no matter what had happened in this life, I loved him.

Getting to his house was an adventure. The coastline was breathtaking, winding roads up mountains, and through a tiny oceanside town. A town so small the radio station announced the visiting relatives of its locals.

When I arrived at his house, I went immediately to his bedroom where he was laying. He had a trachea tube in and was unable to speak above a short whisper. I stood in the doorway of his bedroom and when he turned his head toward me, the expression on his face lit up with every unconditional "I love you" I had ever longed to hear. God did not let my dad leave this earth before we each knew a glimpse of that love from one another. God is so good.

When my earthly father failed, my heavenly Father laid His hands on my shoulders and hid me under His wings in merciful, unconditional love, and protection. When my heavenly Father was bringing my earthly father home, He brought us both under His wing, healed us, loved us, and set us free.

Whatever you need to heal and let go of, God will do it. Ask Him, call His name. He not only will hear you, but also save you, guide you, protect, and fill you with His love. He will redeem the things in your life that caused you pain and use them to lead others in unconditional, Jesus-filled love.

What is God saying to you through this story?

_____

_____

_____

_____

_____

_____

_____

_____

What areas of your heart and life do you need to let Him heal?

_____

_____

_____

_____

_____

_____

_____

_____

Will you trust Him to set you free and redeem your story? Write about it to God, sharing your heart with Him. Remember His hands are on your shoulders to love, guide, heal, and protect you.

_____

_____

_____

_____

_____

_____

Michelle Cochran

———————————————————————————

———————————————————————————

———————————————————————————

A Moment About Mindset

"For as he thinketh within himself, so is he"

- Proverbs 23:7 (ASV)

When I was living alone as a teenager life was very hard. I had worries about paying bills, finishing school, my safety, and having enough to eat at times.

But the prominent thoughts that kept me moving forward were:

1. There is a God.
2. He is aware of me and He speaks to me.
3. There is a purpose for me being on the planet or I wouldn't be on the planet.

Therefore, whatever happens, God knows it and is either doing it or allowing it, so it must be for my good. I thought, 'It must be that He has something to teach me or a way to use me in whatever the given situation was.'

I trusted Him and this reality more than I could see my own hand in front of my face. I fell down and apart many times, but this thinking is what would get me back up and moving every time.

My emotions ran the gamut, from happy to mad at God, constantly. But my emotions were not the most important thing. Trusting Him and His purposes, and focusing on hope and possibility, were the most important things. And still are.

As an aside (soapbox alert), we have been so oversold the notion that we should all be walking around happy, healthy, wealthy, and successful. It has made us afraid to admit we feel any emotions besides happy, healthy, wealthy, and successful. Wisdom and the word clearly teach that the best parts of our growth come from some form of discomfort.

I could easily go on a four page rant on prosperity teachings and how it is taught that we are 'meant to be happy.' UGH! What we are meant to be is holy and happening, and yes there are times of unhappiness in it. But God gives us joy instead and that does not change with circumstance. I have experienced immense joy in times when I had sobbed until my eyes were puffed shut. Or when my heart hurt so bad I wasn't sure I would ever be emotionally healthy again.

So what if we cry, get our hearts broken, get righteously angry, disappointed, rejected, abandon, misunderstood the list goes on and on.

If it doesn't kill us, God will use it to make us stronger. I speak this truth to you in love and confidence, from personal experience. I get a little fired up (if you couldn't tell) about this issue. I know that it sounds a little harsh but I believe the big worldly idea of 'happy' is harmful, and I get all protective and 'mama bear' about it for you. It's false, unrealistic, and deters you from your authentic unfolding in Jesus.

So back to my original point. No matter what comes your way, whether it makes you happy or not, know that God is sovereign and therefore, either doing it or allowing it. And He loves and adores you. He has plans to give you hope and a future (Jeremiah 29:11). But more importantly, He plans to make you holier. Set your mind on that fact and possibility and you will be happier.

Isn't God so smart? Hope and future! A morsel of hope is ten times more powerful than a bucket full of fear. I can't help but think of POW's who sit year after year, captive, in unthinkable circumstances, fearing for their lives. What they go through mentally and emotionally is unimaginable. But when asked what kept them going, you hear them tell stories of the hope they cling to, that they might one day see the ones they love again.

Focus on the hope, the possibility, your personal unfolding in joy and upset. Because He plans to give you a future. He came that you would have joy and have it in full (John 15:11 NAS). He is our reason for living, and nothing on earth, nor the gates of hell shall prevail, when our hope is in Him.

Hope + Focus on God = All things are Possible

In any given situation or circumstance ask God, What do you want me to do or learn in this situation Lord? What are you teaching me about who you are Lord? What is the next thing I can do in obedience?

"Trust in the Lord with all your heart, and do not depend on your own understanding. In all your ways acknowledge him, and he will make your paths straight."

- Proverbs 3:5-6 (ISV)

Please hear my heart in this example, in no way do I intend to dishonor my mother. But to share a real and honest life story, that I pray encourages you. Over the last twenty or so years, my relationship and communication with my mother has been on and off, but mostly off. I love her, but her unhealthiness makes it incredibly difficult to have a relationship of any kind with her. Her physical health is bad and my younger sister has lived with and cared for her, for about twelve years.

In June, of 2015, my sister decided to move out of town with her boyfriend, and left my mother on her own. I started receiving phone calls from their neighbors, telling me my mom was going door to door asking for food, and could I please help her. I was shocked and sad that she would be in that kind of condition and of course, I had to help her.

But I also knew that what helping her meant for me, was countless hours of dealing with and figuring out how government agencies work. It meant walking into unthinkable conditions of filth and unhealthiness. It meant learning all the medications she was on and dispensing them properly. It meant finding her adequate housing and her total dependence on me in every way.

With all of that responsibility comes the emotional, financial, and physical work that in my flesh I did not want to do. I mean I REALLY did not want to do it.

But I knew God was either doing this or allowing it. So there had to be something for my, or our, good in it. I have learned how redemptive and full circle God is, bringing things back around for healing. I hate the circumstances if I am being transparent and honest. But I love Jesus and He loves us both, so I set my eyes on Him. I prayed constantly for Him to give me the strength, patience, and peace to do the work. And I trusted Him, even as I sit here today with anxiety about it, wondering how I will endure it.

My mind wants to say, 'I can't do it.' I want to hide, to distance myself from my mom, because she feels like a weight I can hardly bare. But my hope, trust, and faith is in Christ, and I can do ALL things through Christ who strengthens me (Philippians 4:13 NKJV). And you can do ALL things through Christ who strengthens you.

Here are the steps I have taken each day, since I have taken over her care, to manage my mindset:

1. Every morning the moment I wake up I begin thanking Jesus for who He is and how He works. Knowing that He hides me in the shadow of His wings and that He loves me.
2. I submit myself to Him giving Him all authority over my mind, heart, soul, and body. I ask, "Search me Lord and see if there is any wicked way in me and cleanse me of it."
3. I praise His holy name in prayer and worship.

4. I ask Him to give me peace, joy, love, strength, and mercy for His will to be done through me and through out my day.

5. I whine a little sometimes. I ask, beg, cry, chat, praise, whatever is on my heart. Then I dive into His word, He always meets me (and you) there. He always answers and guides. His love usually leaves me reduced to tears and ready for the day...for the DAY. That is all He asks us to do, one day, this day, thank you Lord!

6. I reach out to my sisters in Christ for prayer and support. Okay and maybe just a little "venting."

I still hate the circumstances, my stomach gets knotted with stress, and I can't care about that. He has me in the palm of His hand and He will take care of me. I will just keep showing up and doing the compassionate work of Christ, because He asks me to. With my mind set on Jesus and bringing Him glory. It's not easy, but it is possible and worth it, because He puts hope and peace in my heart, and His love on my mind.

What if He saves some souls in this process somehow some way? What if He heals her addictions and illness? What if He allows me to show my mother unconditional love to spite my own emotions? She has already asked me how come I am with her, and she is absolutely perplexed by it. That makes two of us. God can truly change anything.

It is nothing short of miraculous and Jesus, that I feel mostly compassion and love for her. He has even given me a few moments of laughter and appreciation, in being reminded. That maybe

I get some of my strength and tenacity from this messy and difficult soul I call mom.

Her behavior is shocking most of the time. She has spirits of addiction, rebellion, and true narcissism. But the good Lord did give her a great sense of humor as a saving grace. Thank you, dear Jesus.

My mind must be set on Jesus, His love for us both, and the things of eternal value. Otherwise I would walk away in a heart beat, it's just so hard.

Whatever God is taking you through or wherever He is leading you. Set your mind on Him and His word, and He will make your path straight and you radiant. A light to the Gentile people, for the sharing of love and the saving of souls. It's all that is truly worth working for anyway, I believe that with all that I am.

"Set your minds on things above, not on earthly things."
                                        - Colossians 3:2 (NIV)

The refiners fire burns hot, but just like Shadrach, Meshach, and Abednego (Daniel 3:23 NIV), who were thrown into the fiery furnace for obeying God. He will walk through the fire with us, He will purify us, and we will emerge without even smelling like smoke! But we must keep our eyes, ears, and minds set on obeying God, for His word tells us that we have the mind of Christ (1 Corinthians 2:16 NIV).

Is God asking or inviting you to do something that seems impossible given emotions or circumstance, If so write about it here.

_____

_____

_____

_____

_____

_____

_____

_____

_____

_____

_____

_____

_____

_____

"We are hard-pressed on every side, yet not crushed; we are perplexed, but not in despair; persecuted, but not forsaken; struck down, but not destroyed."

- 2 Corinthians 4:8-9 (NKJV)

"Yet in all these things we are more than conquerors and gain an overwhelming victory through Him who loved us [so much that He died for us].

- Romans 8:37 (AMP)

Nothing is impossible with God, absolutely nothing. Write a prayer, letter, or Psalm asking God for at least three of His character strengths (i.e. peace, love, mercy, courage) for your current circumstance.

_____
_____
_____
_____
_____
_____
_____
_____
_____
_____
_____
_____
_____
_____
_____
_____

Thank you Lord Jesus that you have your loving arms wrapped tightly around my dear sister. Thank you that you bring hope, redemption, and joy, even in the midst of the refiners fire. Strengthen her faith today Lord, bring encouragement in many forms, but most of all I pray your presence be with her, and she have your mind, Lord. Fill her mind with all things lovely and pure, and give her peace in her heart that she is in the palm of your hand. I know she is precious in your sight and you will walk with and through every trial with her, holding her right hand. Even if her emotions tell her otherwise. Gird her with strength, faith, peace, and trust. I ask this is Jesus' name. Amen

What hope and redemptive story might God be able to author from your current circumstance, knowing He uses ALL things for good for those who love Him?

There is hope that:

_____

_____

_____

_____

_____

_____

_____

_____

_____

_____

_____

_____

_____

Therefore, on the other side of this circumstance, the better story might be:

_____

_____

_____

_____

_____

_____

_____

_____

_____

_____

_____

Lay your circumstance and emotions at His feet and trust Him. He is bigger than all of it, and He has plans to give you hope and a future (Jeremiah 29:11 NIV).

Perfection

I used to wear a tight bun in my hair, dress as nicely as possible, and work hard at staying one step ahead of everyone else in my work and my life. I had a mask of perfection on because I had something to prove. I was determined to excel and achieve!

All I got was tired, lonely, and frustrated always looking for the next bit of recognition for a job well done. What I was really doing was trying to prove I was worthy of being loved. Perfection is a myth and a lie, only God is perfect. While we strive for more of His perfection in us, it is nothing we can ever accomplish or have in the flesh.

Perfection is all about control and proving worthiness. It sucks the life, love, freedom, and creativity out of you. It causes walled-off hearts and arthritis, from gripping the wheel of life so tightly, that nothing of art or beauty can get in. It keeps people at arms length, wears you out in self-sufficiency, and denies your authenticity. Stop doing it, let it go, demand that the spirit of perfection leave you, in Jesus' name.

We have a responsibility, as leaders of light, to connect and share with people well. You can't wrap your arms around people, if your fingers are gripping the wheel of perfection. People best connect with a shared heart, full of what Jesus put there, and expressed in abandon.

In my own wrestling match with perfection, I have found God is not concerned with us getting it all right. He IS our 'right' and righteousness. I believe He is more concerned with our surrendered, brave, and willing hearts, handed completely over to Him. This truth can still make me cry. I have had moments where I sobbed at the realization that I didn't get to have control. There were times in my life when I felt control meant my survival, the need for it felt deeply ingrained in me.

I cried because I was scared, petrified really, of the vulnerability that this walk requires, and I'm still getting used to it. But I kept begging Him to help me surrender it. Because I knew, in surrender, lied truth and freedom. And I wanted that more than my messed up idea of security, in control and perfection.

I want the better story of trust in Jesus, for a fully felt and expressed life. I hope you do too. It is way more fun and adventurous, worth every tear and wrestling match.

Surrender still gets easier every time I pick trusting Him. Everyday I choose to ignore the nag of control and hand Him my heart instead, saying, "Not my will but yours, Lord," it gets easier. And, He makes me stronger, all at the same time.

I still wear a bun in my hair these days, but now it's out of lazy days of writing and house cleaning. It's a loose, curly, wild bun and I even go to the store like that sometimes!

My worth is so tied to the heart of Jesus that while I always want to look my best, I don't care. 'I don't care,' in the sense that I am unattached to perfection. I like my loose, wild, curly bun (that I used to chemically and feverishly straighten). I like my yoga pants and my pencil skirts. But what I like best, is the freedom of knowing that no matter how I'm dressed, or whether or not I achieve anything, God thinks I'm perfect. He thinks you are perfect too, and we both want you to be free in Him. He loves you so much.

Exercise:
Go outside, and if it's warm enough, take your shoes and socks off. Plant your feet in the grass. Feel your feet planted firmly on the ground and the grass touching your feet. This is holy ground, God made this earth, and everything on it.

Close your eyes. Put your hands in front of you like you are gripping a steering wheel. Turn your face up to the sky. Pray, ask God to come and fill and surround you with His love and presence. Let His love and peace fill you up.

Slowly lift one finger at a time off of the 'wheel' saying, "I trust you Lord'" each time you lift a finger off.

When all ten fingers are off the wheel, hold both your hands up in that position of 'both hands off the wheel' about shoulder height. Stand there in that position for a moment, thank God that He promises never to leave or forsake you, and He is trustworthy.

Next, with your hands still up, lift your arms straight up, as if riding a roller coaster hands high in the air. Do you feel a sense of exhilaration and maybe a little scared? Just let yourself notice and feel that for a moment, also noticing, you're okay. Your feet are still firmly planted on God's ground.

Tell God out loud if you are scared, and then ask Him to make you brave and willing to stand there and feel it. Thank Him again that you can trust Him, He will never leave or forsake you, ever.

Now, slowly bring your arms down to shoulder height and open wide, heart lifted toward the sky. Keep your face turned upward, feel the sun, and the wind on your face. Feel God's perfect love radiating on you from above and just receive it, allowing it to fill you completely. Thank the Lord for His perfect, abundant love and grace. His love never runs out, but overflows. He loves you with a jealous and holy love that will find you, keep you, heal you, restore, and redeem you. Let Him. Stand there and let Him love you like that, receive it, believe it, and thank Him. He is every good and perfect gift and He gives Himself to you. Breathe that in from Him, believe Him, love Him.

Doesn't that feel better than a tight bun or a mask? That is who He is, what He is, and how He wants to express love to you and through you. No form of control or unworthiness can stand in the light of that kind of love. Why would we allow ourselves to get in the way or hide His love through us with the silliness of perfection?

We are here for such a short while, sing: "this little light of mine, I'm gonna let it shine..." as messy, and as wild with love, as I possibly can!

Bye Bye perfection!

WATCH THE ACCOMPANYING VIDEO
AT STRONGGIRLPRODUCTIONS.COM

The 'What If' Game

I call the 'what if game' a fear-stopper because it gives us instant perspective about moving forward. It goes like this:

Let's say you are faced with a decision, or an opportunity, to move forward and grow in some area of you life. The idea is exciting, you feel confident that God is in it, and you are ready for a practical next step. Then, you start to think. Ugh, right?

Then you begin to consider all the different scenarios and how they might play out, asking what if this, what if that. You weigh the pros and the cons, you think about all the ramifications of your choice and decision. It can turn into a hamster wheel of confusion, upset, and overwhelm, in the question 'what if.' Before you know it, (in your mind), the world is coming to an end. You ponder, What if I fail, what if I win, what if can't maintain, what if I find out it isn't for me? The list goes on and on.

There is only one answer to these questions: You don't know.

We don't know. So why allow our brains, which is full of old and unhelpful stuff. Not to mention a place darkness loves to contend with us. To make up or give us an answer to a question that only God knows? What we do know is that God is always making us new. He focuses only on where and who we are, and on who He is making us. That is where we should focus also. This approach is God-centered, forward thinking, and creates movement. It also lets God plot the course and write the story.

So, 'what if' you choose to trust Him and enjoy the ride, hands in the air, full and alive with possibility? I call that an adventurous 'what if,' and living the abundant and radiant life He is calling us to.

Let's never pray for the opportunities, the growth, and the decisions to go away. But for greater faith, trust, and courage to take one step into our decisions and see how God shows up to meet us there. He is already there you know. He wants to be something new and something more for you.

He calls Himself "I Am" and He IS. He is never an 'if,' He is solid ground, a rock, a sure thing, a never changing, never leaving, making your path straight God. Rest in the certainty of Him and walk on just believing.

Exercise:

Today, play the 'What If' game, as practice for yourself going forward. The rules are as follows:

1. Every time a situation arises where you start to ponder all the "what if's," you must stop immediately and make your "what if's" positive or even silly.

2. For example: "What if," I don't make that very important meeting on time? Your mind tends to resort to the negatives like: 'I might get fired or lose a client,' or 'I will never ever get another opportunity like this again.' Only today you will choose the positive or even silly like: "If I don't make that very important meeting...," What if I were standing outside in the parking lot and a business card of some random person blew across my feet. What if pick it up and call the person not even knowing why. And that person asks me who I am and what I do for a living. After I tell the person, they say, "Wow we were just talking about needing someone who does exactly what you do, would you come for an interview?" What if you went to the interview and it was a dream job, they hired you, and it was for twice your current salary?

3. For one whole day I want you to practice this mindset and 'What If' game. Did you know that neuroscience has proven you can literally create new pathways in the brain, by consciously and repeatedly choosing new practices or habits?

4. What if you created a new pathway in your brain, that allowed you to choose possibility and positivity, instead of old negative defaults? Choose wild, fun, and adventurous 'What If's,' make them out of your comfort zone and be silly!

5. Take an assessment throughout your day. What are you 'What If-ing,' and are you flipping it to your new positive and adventurous 'What If?'

A few days of practice with this game and I promise you will be living lighter inside and it will radiate outside! Not to mention how your 'world' and what's possible in it, will expand greatly.

What If God, possibility, and adventure ruled your days? What If?

_____

_____

_____

_____

_____

_____

_____

_____

_____

_____

"The steps of a good man (or woman) are ordered by the Lord, And He delights in his way."

- Psalm 37:23 (NIV)

WATCH THE ACCOMPANYING VIDEO
AT STRONGGIRLPRODUCTIONS.COM

Make Noise

"Truth-tellers are the antidote to a world full of facade."

- Michelle Cochran

In so many of the Psalms making a joyful noise is about lifting up joy, praise, and singing to God. It's about love, triumph, and the celebration of who He is and how He works. So much so that it causes a literal eruption of joyful noise and expression.

I can't help but think of the movie "Elf," where Buddy the elf has fallen in love. He comes bursting into his dad's office in a childlike way yelling, "I'm in love, I'm in love, and I don't care who knows it!" All while spinning and donning a large, fluffy, ridiculous looking hat.

Inside of you is a beautiful sound, a joyful noise, sent from heaven ready to erupt in love, playfulness, and intention, to be shared with the world. Your 'sound,' your singing or praise, may emerge in the form of speaking, writing, singing, dancing, teaching, worship, or just being present with those around you.

Like Buddy the elf, when what we have to say, exclaim, or be, comes from authentic love. We don't care who knows it, sees it, or likes it. It is simply an expression of love from God through us.

So, the one thing I hope you take away from this chapter is: regardless of how your sound emerges, you must trust your own unique voice and wisdom. God fashioned it the way He did for His purposes. I just have to say it again, you must trust your own unique voice and wisdom. Why? First, because you are a creation of God's. Wisdom and the Word would dictate that we not deny anything of God. Secondly, sometimes the sound from heaven we are here to make is truth-telling. That's a pill everyone wants and needs, but finds hard to swallow. As leaders of light, we are responsible for telling it in love. There will be a reaction or response. You need to be able to stand in the truth of God's word and what you know, that you know He has given you to say and do. Even if it means things get tense or messy.

We have a responsibility to significantly stand in the love-filled difference God wants to make through us. We must trust Him, trust our unique way of making joyful noise, and stand in the truth of it, firmly planted and 'singing.'

We need more confident truth-tellers willing to share and speak in love. Because truth, spoken in love, from revealed wisdom, lets in more light wherever it is shared, and whatever it sounds like.

In trusting the voice and wisdom God gave you, what if you dared to say what those around you needed to hear the most?

If God is revealing a situation or relationship to you that needs some joyful noise brought to it in the form of loving truth, pray. Ask God to give you wisdom, love, and peace in it. Ask Him to reveal to you, if or how, you should approach the situation, and be obedient to whatever He reveals to you.

He is our God, we are His people, here to bring light to the Gentile people. Here to glorify our Father in heaven and love those He places in our path. Here to lift up a joyful noise of truth, praise, joy, and celebration of the One who causes us to sing like Buddy: "I'm in love, I'm in love and I don't care who knows it!"

Make your truthful, joyful, loving noise...laugh, dance, call darkness what it is to its face. Stand up in the light and joy of your Father, He will guide and protect you. What an audacious way to live and lead, a gift of responsibility and radiance, in beautifully noisy truth.

Your life is a story, here to sing a truth of God, of love, and possibility. Live it to disperse clouds and lies. Live it as a praise to the Author of our faith. Live it marching to the beat of your own drummer, knees lifted high, to leave a really big mark and make the noise that only you can make.

What truth of God, love, and possibility is your soul here to tell?

_____

_____

_____

_____

_____

_____

_____

_____

Are you actively telling it with your life? If so, how?

_____

_____

_____

_____

_____

_____

_____

_____

Fill in the blanks:

My name is:

_____

_____

God put me on this planet to make some truthful, joyful, noise about:

_____

_____

_____

_____

_____

_____

_____

_____

Which glorifies God and serves others

by: _____

_____

_____

_____

_____

_____

_____

Therefore, I will trust the voice, wisdom, and message God gives me or has made me to be and confidently love people with it.

X _____

(Sign here)

My joyful noise is writing. I write to love, to encourage, and even to mouth off a bit about things I see and hear. It is a blessing to be able to do it, but like any personal noise or expression, it is scary business.

Anytime you share your heart and soul with people, you leave yourself wide open for all sorts of harsh and unlovely things. But it's worth it. Because my heart longs to speak things about life on this planet and God, courage, and possibility.

It feels like the thing that I couldn't quit doing, even when fear and insecurity really want me to. And I must make noise, because it comes from a love for my reader, and her precious and powerful heart. I'm in love, I'm in love and I don't care who knows it!

Trust who God has made you to be, and the voice He has given you. People need you to love on them with specifically who you are.

"Instead, speaking the truth in love, we will grow to become in every respect the mature body of him who is the head, that is, Christ."

- Ephesians 4:15 (NIV)

Never Settle

"That the Messiah would suffer and, as the first to rise from the dead, would bring the message of light to His own people and to the Gentiles."

- Acts 26:23 (NIV)

Once you know or at least have the general direction of your calling; the stand you live to take. Never settle for less than everything that it is. Dream it fully, believe God in and for it completely. There is no mistake or coincidence that you love and dream what you love and dream. God put it inside you, trust Him and yourself, and then take at least one action toward it everyday.

Make that call, send that email, write one page, speak up, say something to someone about your dream or idea who can make a difference in its fruition.

When Jesus knew what He had to do, His mission, His calling from the Father, He set His face toward Jerusalem and He walked intentionally to it. He did not look left or right, He set His sights. We must have the same resolve and focus in our callings.

Jesus was pretty clear about following Him. We must be willing, at the very least in our hearts, to leave everything and go where He asks us to go. Sometimes that leaving is physical and sometimes it is emotional, intellectual, or spiritual, but we must be absolutely willing.

Several months ago, I spoke at a professional women's organization. When I shared these very things about not settling and being willing to go where He asks us to. One woman, who happened to be the one that invited me to speak there said, "Well this is great in concept but I have a family." She was a little bothered with this idea and began talking about how she has kids, and a house, a family, she can't just do whatever she feels called to do. Everyone sitting around her nodded in agreement.

We all get scared and defiant because interestingly our minds immediately seem to go to Africa. Like, if I am willing to listen and obey He will surely send me to Africa. I've thought and worried about it too! I am a pansy girly girl who likes a lot of sleep and some Starbucks. So, I kept silent with a loving expression that hopefully asked, is that true?

Two verses came instantly to mind:

"My mother and my brother (family) are those who hear God's word and put it into practice."

- Luke 8:21 (NIV)

"Looking at him, Jesus felt a love for him and said to him, One thing you lack; go and sell all you possess and give it to the poor, and you will have treasures in heaven; and come follow me."

- Mark 10:21 (NASB)

A call from Jesus to leave everything, everyone, and follow Him wherever He leads. This is His command and invitation to us. Comfort and convenience is not a priority, it is tough language, but also a true and sacrificial love.

I have found He has asked me to leave some people and some things behind to go where He was leading me. While it was difficult at first, I found that it was far less dramatic and difficult than the fear would have liked me to think it was, and I have yet to go to Africa. He has our backs but is after our willing hearts. If He brings you to it, He will bring you through it, really.

Each time we are willing to choose God and His call on our lives, we learn that anything or anyone less than Him, will never satisfy us anyway.

God is growing leaders of light because our time on this planet is not going to get easier. He is looking for those who will listen, trust, follow, and obey. So as we shed the shadows of sin and the world His radiance bursts through us as a beacon of hope. Settling for less is simply not an option for those who love Him and are called to light the way.

This is a good fight we're in here. I like the good fight of faith, love, and light, it makes darkness mad and us stronger in Jesus.

God is growing warriors made for a time such as this. Willing warriors of love, who won't stop or settle for less than everything He is making them in this good fight. Let's fight like the girls He's grown us into thus far, and be willing to feel and go through some things, to grow even better and stronger.

We didn't start this fight but we can help finish it well, in love, on fire, and adding to our dear Savior's legacy. The Lord was the first to rise from the dead and proclaim the message of light to the people and we are charged with the same task.

"It is no small thing that you should be My Servant to raise up the tribes of Jacob, and to restore the preserved ones of Israel; I will also give you as a light to the Gentiles, that you should be My salvation to the ends of the earth."
- Isaiah 49:6 & Acts 13:47 (NKJV)

Jesus did it and so must we.

"And as many as had been appointed to eternal life believed."
- Acts 13:48 (NKJV)

If I were continuing that last verse (Acts 13:48) in my own words, for this context I would add, "And accepted their privilege and responsibility with humility, never settling for a lesser light or proclamation, than the one given to them by God."

Never ever settle for less than everything God is making you, it is yours to be, yours to love and lead in, and how we win the good fight.

Prayer

It Heals.
It Saves. It Moves.
It Transforms.
It Leads.
It Protects.
It Provides.
It Delivers.
It Forgives.
It Lifts.
It Reveals..It Loves, Pray.

"It shall come to pass that before they call, I will answer, and while they are still speaking, I will hear."

- Isaiah 65:24 (NKJV)

Rely

A love journey of any kind is wrought with every emotion, lots of twists, turns, highs and lows. The love journey of leading, is no different. And when we walk this leadership path, we must have total reliance on God.

I am not talking about the general knowing as Christ followers that we are to be reliant on Him. I am talking about minute detail reliance. For example, one day when I suddenly got a call to attend a last minute business meeting. I had only one pair of pants dry cleaned and ready to wear. And I needed a very specific pair of underwear to wear with those pants. I know, to much information, bear with me.

As I headed for the dresser drawer, with beads of nervous sweat on my upper lip, I was worried my underwear would not be there. I began to pray with every step toward the drawer, "Lord, you are in the details, please oh please let those underwear be in that drawer."

I opened the drawer, and not only were they in there, they were laying right on top, as if God were saying, "Here you go, I take care of everything." I literally danced around for a moment in a singsongy performance of gratitude. Phil, my cat (named by my teenage son), stared on with a very concerned expression.

"Thank you Lord, you are so good, and awesome, and you always take care of me, you love me and I love you." Weird I know, but I believe He delights in our total reliance in everything, the good stuff, the hard stuff, and even the mundane.

I don't think He numbered the hairs on our head (Luke 12:7) because He had nothing better to do. He cares about every detail of who we are, and our lives.

You know that parking spot that opened up at the store right when you needed it to? Remember when that check came in the mail, or that encouragement that happened right when you needed it?

All good and perfect things come down from the Father of lights (James 1:17 NIV), and when we learn to rely on Him as our sole source and the source of our soul, we are practicing powerful, underwear providing faith! I created a little acronym (can you tell I kinda like acronyms) for the word rely, in case you are like me and can use a tool to help you remember.

Rest in God.
Expect His love & answer.
Listen for His voice & direction.
Yield EVERYTHING in obedience to what He tells you.

Then take one step in the direction of His instruction to you. It is simple and just requires a lot of practice so I hope the acronym helps.

He is the vine, we are the branches (John 15:5), apart from Him we truly can do nothing of eternal value. He is Jehovah Jireh, our provider (Genesis 22:14).

RELY on God in everything, for everything, with every bit of your heart, soul, mind, and strength. (Luke 10:27, Mark 12:30, Deuteronomy 6:5)

He is our inner-wear, that provides our outer armor, and yes, even our under-wear. RELY on God.

Can you think of any ways in which you may have become too self-reliant instead of relying on God?

Write a few them here:

_____

_____

_____

_____

_____

_____

_____

"If you abide in Me, and My words abide in you, you will ask what you desire, and it shall be done for you."

- John 15:7 (NKJV)

Look back at the list you just made and ask the Lord how you might take steps toward releasing your self-reliance, and how to move toward relying more on Him. Use the RELY formula/ acronym above as a guide. You can journal that here.

_____

_____

_____

_____

_____

_____

_____

_____

_____

_____

_____

_____

_____

List your thoughts, feelings, and the Lord's answer, your impressions and ideas here.

_____

_____

_____

_____

_____

_____

_____

_____

_____

_____

_____

_____

_____

"And God is able to make all grace abound toward you, that you, always having all sufficiency in all things, may have an abundance for every good work."

- 2 Corinthians 9:8 (NKJV)

Others

"I find that I am the most frustrated and stuck, when I am thinking the most, about myself."

- Michelle Cochran

The sun does not shine for its own benefit, and its rays do not radiate inward. God spoke the sun into existence for a purpose. It rises every day, provides, and sets. So must we.

We live in a culture that teaches us to rise, get up every day, go out in self-focus and get, chase, have. Then rest...but only as long as absolutely necessary, and then do it all again the next day.

Organically, like the sun, we are made as servant-leaders. We are created from God to serve a purpose that provides for others, rest, and do all that again the next day.

When our service is bursting outward from a full heart of love and light. We usually find that we wind up with everything we were chasing anyway...or even better.

We will be effective as leaders of light when we master the reality that we are on this earth to serve. To serve God, a purpose, and others, with our whole hearts alive and ablaze in who He has made us, for the benefit of others.

That's the best strategy or marketing plan you will ever receive. Here is a little equation to help you remember it. (see how geeky I am that I love these little tools that help me).

Do your thing + with great love + in service + now = Radiant Servant Leadership.

Here's to you shining in beautiful service!

"I beseech you therefore, brothers, by the mercies of God, that you present your bodies a living sacrifice, holy, acceptable to God, which is your reasonable service."

- Romans 12:1 (AKJV)

Exercise:

I believe we learn best when we live something. So this is an exercise for those who might like to test this theory out for themselves in a daily experiment.

Take one week, and for that entire week, be completely self-focused. Worry only about your needs, your wants, and your desires. One week where the whole time, you do nothing but think about yourself.

Right about now all the moms are saying, "Yeah right, like I could really do that when I have kids!" And probably the rest of you are almost laughing at the absurdity, given that as women, we don't like to think about ourselves.

This should be a pretty good indicator of how holistically unnatural it truly is. So, you guessed it, I am not serious. It even gave me a knot in my stomach to type that. We are not made for self-focus, period.

So now, go out and flagrantly bless people with your time, love, gifts, and talents. You both will be hugely blessed...and maybe stop for a Starbucks somewhere along the way.

"Do nothing from selfishness or empty conceit, but with humility of mind regard one another as more important than yourselves."
                                                    - Philippians 2:3 (NASB)

Comparing

"It takes a holy bravery to live as an individual."

- Michelle Cochran

I scrolled through Pinterest the other day, enjoying all the quotes and sentiments about comparison, as I prepared to write this piece for you. I loved a lot of what I found there and even had a little 'aha moment.' The aha moments for me usually begin with a question like: 'where did the idea of comparing ourselves come from in the first place?'

I'm sure I could trace the history and reasons and it would be interesting. But in our current culture, I believe marketing psychology is a primary culprit. Its job is to intentionally convince you that in some way you are not enough, you do not have enough, and that you must have whatever they are pandering, to be happy and whole.

The greatest favor you could do for yourself is to unplug from the rhetoric. Stop listening to it, or giving validity to it, and start to have an awareness that almost every bit of media is designed to tell you how 'not enough' you are.

Why allow ourselves to be barraged with a message like that? Particularly when our own insecurities will do a perfectly fine job of that all on their own. We fall victim to the thinking that if their messages are everywhere, it is 'popular,' and everyone is buying into it. Then what they are saying must be 'right' and just what we need. Right? Wrong.

All this scenario does is start the process of comparison in your mind. It has you asking yourself how you measure up to what is 'popular' and 'right,' and puts you in perpetual chasing and comparing. Sounds like the work of darkness to me. This is a great distraction from the beautiful organic truth of who God made you and the fact that you are holistically enough.

There is nothing 'out there' better than what God put in you to be, nothing! It is never who you are that will hold you back, it is always who you think you are not.

What if you chose to only listen to who God says you are? What if you spent less of your time in front of a screen and more time exploring the truth of who He says you are?

I tried out these questions for myself and I found there are typically three versions of ourselves. There is the 'you' the world sees, the 'you' that you see yourself as, and the 'you' that God sees and says you are. The first two keep me stuck in insecurity and render me ineffective. The third keeps me moving forward, hopeful, alive in possibility, and frankly not caring much what anyone else is doing, or saying.

It truly takes a holy bravery to live as your organic God-made self. The colorful masterpiece that only God can paint and author.

It can tick people off sometimes and rub them the wrong way. Individuality freaks people out. When you are not conforming to what's culturally popular, you wake people up from a robotic sleep-walk and it's unsettling. Jesus was very good at this.

Light leaders, like Jesus, do not compare themselves to others and fit in a popular mold, they change things with their presence. Yes, it's hard, it's scary, but it's also adventurous, mischievous, and full of possibility. It is desiring to let Jesus love people uniquely through you, more than you desire the security and comfort of fitting in.

How exhausting to have to be always 'checking your side mirrors' to see where your lane is and how you are measuring up. Especially when Jesus has a scenic path and story already marked out for you. Choose Him, be you, stop looking around.

Most of our fumbling and frustration comes from one fundamental thinking: that somehow 'I am not enough.' How that must grieve God's heart to see His beloved, His cherished and treasured people, doubting how He made them and wasting their potential.

I watched a story on tv about Jesus' life on earth recently. There was the scene where Jesus is sitting on a hillside overlooking the city of Jerusalem, with tears rolling down His beautiful face in grief, for the lost potential of that city and its people, His people.

I could feel my own heart breaking, as I cried too, and right along with Him. I wanted to cry out, "Do we not know who and what we are?" "Do we not know the Holy Spirit of God almighty lives in us?" If we believe that truth, then what on earth are we doing looking around?

We have work to do and we have no time or need to wonder what others think or say about us. We are not wimps that we should wither and worry. We are warriors of love and light. Set to rule, change and stir things, raise awareness and few eyebrows about who God is. Not sit stuck in who we are not.

Let's not get sucked into or concern ourselves with what the current culture wants to sell us as an idea of what is acceptable, good, or right.

Let's lay down any thoughts or feelings of "not good enough" at the feet of Jesus in repentance and ask for healing. Let's be the simple, brighter example of what is acceptable, good, and right. However God chooses to express it through us. For He is altogether lovely inside you. When He speaks or moves through you, it is enough, just the way it is...just the way you are.

The only two places you should ever look to compare yourself is in your heart and His eyes.

Comparing cannot live where grace resides and you are God's grace in motion. Go love people with a wild holy bravery and I promise you, comparing yourself to anyone or anything, will quickly become a thing of the past.

Bravery

"Shall I lead into the battle fronts an army of weeping women? Shall I ask the faint-hearted to war?"

- Frances J. Roberts, Come Away My Beloved

Being brave can mean different things to different people. But God lets us know that He is with us and has commanded us, commanded us, not to be afraid. That should be definition and reason enough to be strong and of good courage.

According to dictionary.com bravery means: brave spirit or conduct.

I believe, that it is any time we trust God well enough, to do the harder thing, to get to a better thing.

I love stories of bravery the most because they are just that, examples of everyday people, doing harder things for the better things. Heroes and heroines willing to push through and persevere in life altering circumstances for a greater good. What a thrill to watch, and what hope it brings! That is what you are doing when you are brave in your life story. You bring a thrill of hope.

What brave story will your life tell to those who are watching it?

You already know you are chosen to be a light in this world, so what stops you from being brave in it?

Would it really matter if you failed at what you chose to show up in and do? Would you really choose differently anyway?

I'm guessing you would still choose to do whatever "it" is for you. Because if God has called you to be or do something, you simply can't deny it. He who has begun a work in you will be faithful to complete it (Philippians 1:6), no matter if it looks like failure or success.

You may be asking yourself, "What is 'it' for me, exactly?" It is the thing you keep coming back to, or is right under your nose, nagging you to pay attention to it. It feels like an authentic 'yes' in your spirit when you see, hear, or notice it.

It is sometimes an ordinary, everyday, 'yes' that is sacrificial and loving. It is courage rising up in one person to stand up for another. It is the sharing of a personal expression to uplift, encourage, and inspire.

It is you, being willing to just say yes and trust God, no matter what it is. Big or small, loud or quiet, simple or profound, just saying yes and doing it. Every time you do, it gives hope and permission, blesses others, and makes you stronger in your own heart and faith. God is just, poetic, and beautiful like that. When we step up and out in faith, love, and bravery we may be scared to death. But on the other side of it, are blessings for everyone, including you.

We always need more brave people in the world, but this is a time for brave love. Its time for courageous expressions and sacrifice, that intentionally show the world, that we believe God and love people.

The best way to start being brave in love is to practice, practice, practice.

What is one simple thing God has been talking to you about that you can go and do in brave love today? Then just like shampoo, rinse and repeat, everyday.

One simple act of a brave love today, makes a mighty brave warrior of love tomorrow.

A prayer: Father, we are at a place in your beautiful love story that calls me to be brave. Thank you that you chose to put me here on this planet for such a time as this, it is certainly by your divine design. I don't want to shrink from this challenge Lord. You have made me a warrior of light, a city on a hill, a beacon of hope. You fashioned me in my mother's womb that even I cannot deny that I am chosen, liberated, redeemed, and free. Father, help me to walk in the confident freedom of your love, which makes me brave. Dear Lord, please forgive my unbelief, disobedience, or self-focus. Father, break the chains of timidity that can grip my heart. Your love makes me strong and brave, You are mine and I am Yours. Come and express Your love and will through me Lord. Help me to be brave love in action, all glory to God, in Jesus name I pray. Amen

Exercise:

It's your turn. Write your prayer to the Lord. Express, confess, and share with Him everything that you are feeling about being brave love to others. Then ask Him to heal, fill, and redeem whatever He needs to, to make you a greater reflection of His love and light.

_____

_____

_____

_____

_____

_____

_____

_____

_____

_____

"For God did not give us a spirit of timidity, but a spirit of power, of love and of self-discipline."

- 2 Timothy 1:7 (NIV)

"Haven't I commanded you: be strong and courageous? Do not be afraid or discouraged, for the Lord your God is with you wherever you go."

- Joshua 1:9 (HCSB)

Who will be impacted by your bravery?

_____

_____

_____

_____

_____

_____

_____

How will they benefit from your brave love?

_____

_____

_____

_____

_____

_____

_____

_____

_____

"What lies behind us and what lies before us are small matters compared to what lies within us."

- Ralph Waldo Emerson

The presence and power of almighty God live in you, go and live like it. It will bless those watching with hope, permission, and a bravery of their own.

Game On

We do not war against flesh and blood, but against powers and principalities (Ephesians 6:12), when we take a stand as light and love. When we own our power and authority, we will be met with resistance and conflict.

Have you ever had a time where you have taken a stand, or committed to growth or moving forward in some way? Whether it was in educating yourself, putting yourself 'out there' in some way, or speaking up. And when you did it, wham! Something happened that either subtly distracted you or flat out sacked you. Like you are the quarter back holding the football, and you get taken out from the sideline, and didn't even see it coming?

Darkness hates you. It wants to steal, kill, and destroy (John 10:10) every dream, passion, and love-filled contribution you are called to make. Those are pretty strong words (from scripture) describing what we must deal with. We will get attacked and knocked down at times, particularly when we are stepping up as light.

We usually don't see or expect it and it can come from the unlikeliest of places. We get disappointed, our hearts broken, and usually a really good lesson if we receive it. We just have to know it is part of the spiritual battle we are engaged in. Make no mistake, it is a battle we are engaged in.

We are fighting for the hearts, minds, and souls of every man, woman, and child on this earth. It is 'game on!' While that is a God-sized task, each individual lighting up and doing their part in the body is what accomplishes it. We will take a few right hooks and sacks, we'll get our feelings hurt from people and places we don't expect, and we'll want to quit. But God never brings any of us to or through a good fight without a purpose and a plan.

We may find ourselves on the mats, down for the count, with darkness counting four, three, two...and maybe not until the last count of one, God steps in and says, "Get up." He causes us to rise up again, somehow, someway, and we are victorious in Him!

He who has begun a work in you will be faithful to complete it (Philippians 1:6). He is victorious, He never loses. Ever. When God sends you into a good fight of faith, He has the victory already planned. Remember, that we fight from victory, not for it.

Let's not walk in fear of falling or even getting knocked down. We're assured it will happen, but so what really. It hurts for a moment, but He is worth it, and He makes it so worth it to us. We become stronger, more brave and like Him. I don't say this lightly, or to come off as being trite, but from experiencing dark depths.

There is a saying; "God will never give you more than you can handle." I don't like that saying, because I don't think it's true.

I searched the Scriptures to find that saying and all I came up with was 1 Corinthians 10:13 (NWT) it says, "No temptation has come upon you except what is common to men. But God is faithful, and he will not let you be tempted beyond what you can bear, but along with the temptation he will also make the way out so that you may be able to endure it."

This verse deals with temptation, speaking about when we are being tempted to sin, that he will not let us be tempted beyond what we can bear, by giving us a way out of it. A way to not sin, by giving us a way to choose what is right.

I have lived moments and seasons where I felt the circumstances of my life were more than I could ever bear or recover from. Moments of anguished hopelessness and depression that I literally begged God to take my life.

I was in what is referred to as; 'the dark night of the soul.' While I believe that God will never allow us to be tempted beyond what we can handle. I believe He most certainly allows us circumstances we can't handle. Why? Why would He do that?

Because that is precisely when we call His name, reach out to Him, realize our need and dependence on Him. Precisely when we understand we cannot do this life, nor are we doing this life, on our own.

So much so, that even as I were lying there in bed wishing for death. Absolutely unable to muster a mere thought of hope, unable to call on Him because darkness enveloped me. He used that circumstance of 'more than I could handle,' to reveal Himself to me, as light. If I weren't physically, mentally, and emotionally 'leveled' or knocked down. I would not have paid attention to Him.

Oh, He will allow us more than we can handle on our own, but only and always for our good. If need be, He'll chase us right into the depths of darkness to haul us out, raise us up, redeem, restore, and renew us. Like only a loving and powerful Father can.

Sometimes I believe we get 'knocked down' for the purpose of choosing for ourselves; a test of faith. Will you rise up and fight for your life and given path or quit? It begs the question in that moment: Which is harder, to fight or to quit? We never do either one alone, but which will you choose?

Are you ready to find out?

If yes, then 'game on' world, for we are torch carriers, message bringers, light bearers, truth-tellers, love expressions breathed by God. We fall down, but we rise up, we do not quit. For He is our God and we are His people, here to lead, win souls, change things, and be radiantly victorious! Praise Jesus!

The Remnant

"The daughter of Zion is left like a shelter in a vineyard, Like a watchman's hut in a cucumber field, like a besieged city. Unless the Lord of hosts had left us a few survivors, we would be like Sodom, we would be like Gomorrah."

- Isaiah 1:8-9 (NASB)

I am nothing from nowhere really, an ordinary woman in a small town. Yet there is a sunrise in my soul, put there by God. It is the Holy Spirit and He wants to burst forth through every pore in my body as love, light, and liberation for those around me.

As I look around at the current landscape, I know that I'm not the only one. I can see there is a powerful remnant that God is cultivating and calling forth, to lead the way, and it is a thrill to watch.

Much like the movie, I call this remnant 'divergents,' because the definition of a divergent is: to differ in opinion, character, and form, having no finite limits, according to dictionary.com.

We are divergents in Jesus, differing in form, character, and opinion from the world and its expectations. We have no finite limits in Jesus, as He is limitless.

But what we do have, is a bit of an identity crisis. As God authors and fashions us into warriors of light, we have to leave who we were behind. Possible very quickly, if your experience has been anything like mine.

It prompts questions like: God who are you making me into? What exactly are you asking me to do? What is this new role and path you are putting me on, and who do I need to be to walk in it?

Sometimes, it is even just a shift or amplification of the place we are already in, not necessarily a big change. For others it can be a total life overhaul.

The answers may vary for each of us. But what I know for sure is that if we keep asking, keep following, and seeking Jesus. He will get us on the straight and unique path He has for us. The key is to stay in peace, patience, and persistence of the One authoring the change.

Seven years ago, when God began authoring a new storyline for me. I was absolutely certain it was for counseling or coaching full time. I am talking about heels-totally-dug-in certain, and I was so wrong. It turns out He wants to use the one simple thing I dearly love, words and writing. But I gave almost no credence to it.

He is making me a better writer and teacher, and it has made me sit with my head cocked to the side like a small dog, perplexed.

I'm actually in awe that the answer was quite simple and under my nose...it usually is.

But while the answer was simple and under my nose, it wasn't easy. He had to wrestle my own thinking and ideas out of my hands. I regularly pray to get better about this, I am so thick-skulled it's ridiculous. I had to believe Him, that the thing He was showing me and steering me toward was true and real. This required more trust, surrender, and vulnerability. Then came the revelation, ownership, and embodiment of my new identity in Him.

Wow, what a place of freedom and exhilaration it is, this new identity in Him! It is so worth every bit of struggle, tears, wondering, and surrender.

I think of the process or experience as sort of a 'spiritual boot camp.' A breaking down and a letting go of an old identity, to be built up in a new one, a better, stronger version of the one you were before. With your gifts, talents, and possibly new skills amplified and brought to the forefront.

No matter where we are on our path with Him. We must absolutely trust God and our identity, as divergent's in Him, to be effective as leaders of light.

The reality is we are afraid of our own identity as individuals. I feel like that should be said again: we are afraid of our own identity as individuals. And in order to lead anything or anyone well, or contribute in a significant way, we must know and lead ourselves well, first.

I could spend a lot of time talking about fears and insecurities and how they get in the way, but why give them energy or airtime? We have holy work to do, and while they need addressing, I like Jesus's example of always focusing on making the new man or woman.

We want to fit in, be accepted and loved, and so we work to fit in. But Jesus did not fit in, and neither do we. Light is disruptive, beautiful, truthful, nurturing, it exposes, its presence is poetic, unique, and lovingly intentional. How do you put that in a mold of conformity?

How He makes us different is how He makes us effective. We must believe that.

We all want to join in, be a part of something, but none of us should fit into a mold. You cannot put the wind in a box and you cannot put the burning heart and love of Jesus in one either. It's free, wildly expressive, and controlled by the Father alone. So is the powerful individual, and remnant of light in the world, you.

Love who God has made you thus far, allow Him to author new storylines through you, and embrace the leader He is making you through it. He tells us again and again throughout scripture, "Don't be afraid, only believe." (Mark 5:36 HCSB) Let's not just act like Christians, but live like loved believers.

As He is, so are we, in this world. We are called to be Jesus' hands, feet, and ambassadors of love and light, just as He was. He knew His identity in the Father He did and spoke just what the Father told him. He hung out with misfits and sinners. He stirred things up and challenged conventional thinking. All while He radiated peace, love, truth, mercy, and grace. Even when He was grossly misunderstood, lied about, slandered, denied, rejected, humiliated, lonely, and killed.

Are you, daughter of light, ready to embrace your identity in Jesus? Are you willing to live and lead as an individual in Christ? To stand as a part of the holy, chosen, powerful remnant on earth? Will you take His hand and walk in peace, belief, and authority?

Will you use your time, gifts, talents, and calling to edify the body of believers and church of Jesus Christ?

You are differing in opinion, form, and character with no finite limits in Jesus. You are the divergent remnant of Jesus Christ on this earth. Believe it, believe Him, lead like it by example and in every good work, that it would glorify your Father in heaven.

Exercise:
Throughout scripture God gave people He was using a new name. For example he changed Simons' name to Peter, and called him a rock on which He would build His church (Matthew 16:18). As God authors a new storyline of leadership through your individual and unique life, and you welcome and embrace it. Choose a name for yourself, that represents who He is calling you to be and name the new role.

(example: Simons' name changed to Peter, and his new role went from both fisherman to fisher of men, and rock)

Your current name:

_____

Your new name:

_____

The name of your new role:
(example: mine went from 'counselor' to writer and teacher)

_____

_____

_____

_____

Do not be afraid, just believe, and embrace it. Focus on the new creature God is making you for His purposes. Leave old thinking, ideas, and expectations at His feet. He adores you, fill up in Him. Live like the woman, the individual, He made you to be. It's okay, really.

Was this difficult? Did you skip it? Give yourself time to pray and sit with this. Come back to it if you need to, God's pace is always peace.

In the movie Divergent, the ones who are divergent are the problem. They are the ones that must be eliminated in order to keep the cultures definition of peace. In the movie's sequel,

Insurgent, (spoiler alert) we learn that divergents were not only 'not the problem.' But they are actually the answer, the solution.

I believe the same is true in our current culture's story. The divergents, the ones called, chosen, distinct in character, form, and opinion with no finite limits in Jesus, are indeed the answer. Your distinction makes you glorious, dangerous, and very necessary. Lead in your divergence.

"Who will rise up for me against the evildoers? or who will stand up for me against the workers of iniquity?"

- Psalm 94:16 (AKJV)

"Also I heard the voice of the Lord saying: Who should I send? Who will go for us? I said, Here am I. Send me."

- Isaiah 6:8 (NKJV)

Joy

"For the joy of the Lord is your strength"

- Nehemiah 8:10 (NIV)

How often do you laugh? I mean laughing until there is no sound, and tears are streaming your face, laugh? Do you romp, or skip, or just lose yourself in the silliness of a moment?

When we see people do it, we are lifted, reminded of the importance of being childlike in our joy, and the blessings it brings. And secretly, we wish we would let ourselves go, to feel and express joy like that.

How about today? How about laughing, or playing a joke, or just remembering a moment in your life where you were care free in joy?

The bible tells us that the joy of the Lord is our strength. How we delight in Him, and He delights in us, gives us that strength. It says that He came so we would have joy and have it overflowing. Joy is very important. Jesus said so.

Even if weeping endures for a night, joy comes in the morning (Psalm 30:5 AMP), like the sunrise, it brings hope for a better day. Joy is so very important.

Joy is Jesus. Fill up in Jesus always, and soak in His abundant joy. Then just see if you don't feel like laughing, sharing, skipping, singing, and loving people silly. Loving people joyfully is unbelievably important.

Joy is a gift, receive it.

Joy is a weapon, use it.

Joy is a compass, follow it.

Joy is who you are in Him, and it makes you radiant, be it.

Sunbeams & Seymour St.

About a year and a half ago, while I was trying to figure out what this book was supposed to be and asking God whom He was making me. I sat staring out the window in my bedroom thinking, searching. And then I asked, "God, what is this book and what do you want me to do?"

I immediately flashed to Seymour St. where I lived alone at sixteen years old, and I heard, "Go and walk it." In my usual stubborn and thick-skulled nature I thought I knew why. So I replied, "I know. You want me to see and be grateful for how far You've brought me, and I get that." What a total joy I must be to teach and parent.

So, I went back to thinking, struggling, and trying to figure it out. Only in a lot of my quiet moments I would keep flashing back to Seymour St. and hearing God say, "Go and walk it," which I still did not do. When I say I am thick-skulled, think very large boulder on my shoulders.

But one morning, I believe it was spring-time, (I love Spring-time), the weather was lovely so I decided to go to the park for a walk. After my walk I was driving home and came to a stop light. It so happened that I was right at the intersection where I would need to turn right to get to Seymour St.

As I sat there, the same words flashed about Seymour St. "Go and walk it," and I said, "Okay Lord, let's see what you have for me." As I turned the corner and headed toward Seymour St. I heard a voice in my spirit say, "Boots on the ground."

If you happened to watch the auditions for American Idol a couple of seasons ago. There was an elderly gentlemen who auditioned with his own original song, "Pants on the Ground." I found it hilarious and so fun, and the "boots on the ground" message I was getting, came in the tune of this man's "Pants on the Ground" song. It played over and over in my mind as I drove there..."boots on the ground, boots on the ground..." slightly annoying really. But He got the point across the 'boulder' on my shoulders.

I knew He wanted me to park my car and literally walk Seymour St. I figured it would be safe since it was the middle of the day. While I really don't like going back there, I had a sense of adventure with Jesus, feeling He had something to reveal.

I arrived and found on the corner of Seymour St. a brand new doctors office, I pulled into it and parked. It sits about two blocks from where I used to live in that studio apartment, in the upper part of that old house.

I was shaking, I had butterflies in my stomach, and I said, "Okay Lord, let's do this." I started up the street toward my old place. On my left was another new doctors office, Dr. Israel. Not kidding! On my right was an elementary school that was seriously run down when I lived on the block. Now it had all brand new windows and was landscaped with flowers.

129

I couldn't believe what I was seeing. I kept walking in nervous anticipation and even gratitude for how that place had sustained me at a time when I needed sustaining very badly.

I came upon a bright red-haired woman, sitting on a long canopied swing in the yard, rocking whimsically with her toes in the air. All around her were brilliantly colored flowers, she and the flowers radiated warmth.

I said, "Hello, how are you?"

She said, "Just fine dear. It's so beautiful out today."

I chuckled in agreement and said, "Yes, it is."

I kept walking up the block and there it was, my old place. I stared at it so full of gratitude I had to fight back tears. Then I noticed a car sitting at the end of the drive with a young man in it.

The car was packed full of junk. It hadn't been washed in a long while and some pretty heavy beats were thumping out of its windows. I walked around to the driver side, slightly unsure of how to address this person. But when he saw me he turned down his music, smiled and said, "What can I do for ya?"

I smiled back and asked, "Do you by chance know the name of the gentlemen that owns this house? I used to live here a long time ago, and I would really like to find and thank him."

He said, "No, ma'am I don't know I am just visiting my friend who lives here, but you can go and ask my friend."

I declined, but thanked him for his time. He said, "Is there anything else I can do to help you." 'What is going on?' I thought and said chuckling once again, "No thank you, I'm good." He nodded and pulled away. On the walk back to my car the birds were singing loudly. I caught a glimpse through the houses of a small revitalized park, on the next street over. I was in awe, filled with waves of gratitude and love, which was so surprising to me.

I drove home perplexed and in silence, with a slight smile on my face that felt like peace. I retreated to my bedroom, aka prayer closet, when I got home. I returned to the chair in the corner by the window where I had looked out and had 'asked' God before.

I said, "God what was that experience?"

God laid on my heart the words; "I transformed it, just like I transformed you."

As I sat there I saw a picture of Jesus hovering over Seymour St. shrouded in brilliant light, with His arms outstretched. He took my hand and we walked off of Seymour St. together, different, stronger. With a sense that we were going to go to work in the world, together. I cried until I was out of sound and tears.

I cried out of awe and gratitude. I cried out of repentance for not having walked it when He told me to, and for the revelation that He not only makes all things new, He restores all that was lost.

My radiant friend and pastor,Tracy, recalled this verse recently, and it is so fitting.

"So I will restore to you the years the swarming locust has eaten"
- Joel 2:25a (AKJV)

He is coming to make the whole earth new. He will transform us and it, restoring everything that was lost. He is coming.

Until then, we have work to do, and He teaches us exactly how to do it in the beautiful verses of Isaiah chapter 58: 6-12 (The Voice):

"What I want in fasting and worship is this: to liberate those tied down and held back by injustice, to lighten the load of those heavily burdened, to free the oppressed and shatter every type of oppression."

"Worship or a fast for me involves sharing your food with people who have none, giving those who are homeless a space in your home, giving clothes to those who need them, and not neglecting your own family."

"Then, oh then, your light will break out like the warm, golden rays of the rising sun; In an instant, you will be healed. Your rightness will precede and protect you; the glory of the Eternal will follow and defend you."

"Then when you do call out, My God, Where are You?" The Eternal One will answer, "I am here, I am here. If you remove the yoke of oppression from the downtrodden among you, stop accusing others, and do away with mean and inflammatory speech."

"If you make sure that the hungry and oppressed have all that they need, then your light will shine in the darkness, and even your bleakest moments will be bright as a clear day."

"The Eternal One will never leave you; He will lead you in the way you should go...And all around, others will call you repairer of broken down walls." Rebuilders of home and community.
- Isaiah 58: 6-12 (The Voice)

I believe God is walking off of every one of our personal "Seymour Streets" with us, hand in hand, along side each one of us who call Him Lord and Savior.

How has God transformed you? How can you use it to light the way for others? Write about that here.

_____

_____

_____

_____

_____

_____

_____

_____

_____

_____

_____

When you use it for the building up of His Kingdom, He promises your light will break forth like the dawn. Your life will be bathed in sun and God will guide you always. He will satisfy your needs in the emptiest of places. Your healing will quickly appear, your righteousness will go before you, and the glory of God behind you. You will call and God will answer, you will cry for help and God will say, "Here I am." (Isaiah 58) Believe Him.

I am choosing to intentionally live this fight and love-filled adventure with Jesus, as He still makes me new every day. Walking with those He is calling up and out to lead. We have a difference to make, a race to finish, glory to bring to God, and a way to pave for His return, loving lots of souls along the way.

This is an intense time of choice and obedience in history. A time for those who know and hear their Shepherd's voice, to lose their lives, their selves, and their ways for His.

"But the people who know their God shall become strong, and carry out great exploits. And those of the people who understand shall instruct many."

- Daniel 11:32-33 (NKJV)

About a year ago now, I was at my bank standing at the counter speaking with the teller, when I heard my name called just to my left. I turned to see who it was and there stood my friend's mother, the one I had lived with when I was sixteen. The one whom had asked me to leave her home, and in so doing I wound up on Seymour St.

I instantly swelled with joy and relief and with a huge smile on my face I called out her name in return, she seemed surprised and timid. I motioned 'just a minute' with my finger and asked if I could talk to her outside, she nodded in agreement.

We walked outside the bank and she stared at me in curiosity as I told her how happy I was to see her. She said she was happy to see me too, but wondered why I was glad to see her?

I told her that I had worried for years, that I would never get the chance to tell her how grateful I was to her, for taking me into her home and caring for me for a time. Her chest and shoulders sank as she stared in disbelief at what I was saying.

She said, "Oh, I am so relieved you feel that way, I didn't know what you would think of me?" I began to recant to her all of the fun and beautiful memories I had of my time with her and my friend.

The time the three of us laid in the sun on her boyfriends boat dock with Cindy Lauper crooning "time after time..." My friend and I laughing as we tried to sing the words to her mom before Cindy could, so she could sing along in time with Cindy on the radio.

Or when she made my friend and I watch the presidential debate on t.v. so we could have an 'informed opinion.' When all we cared about was who was the cutest and what they were wearing.

We both laughed and enjoyed reliving those moments and I said, "I just want you to know how grateful I am to you and what a difference you made in my life, thank you so much."

I saw a deep sadness in her eyes and I was puzzled. She took a heavy deep breath and shared some difficulties she was having personally and relationally in her life. My heart was heavy for her in that moment, but she said, "I needed this today, I am so glad I saw you."

I could see that in that moment she desperately needed to know she mattered and made a difference somehow. God is so loving, so good and full circle. As He personally and spiritually walks me off the street that leaving her home had brought me to live on. He used it to heal and bring hope to us both.

God once graced me with His presence as a light, a sunbeam that broke through darkness, and commanded, "Get up." He is asking all of His daughters to get up, to pull on their combat boots under their silken, lacy, bejeweled wedding gown, and fight the good fight of faith.

He's asking us to rise, radiate, and reign, like the sun, like the Son, and like a girl who's heart is on fire for her bride-groom, and the world He came to save. For we are here for only a short while, but to leave a long legacy of love on fire.

He's moving, He's transforming, He is bringing full circle and to fruition His incredible love story. For He is sunbeams and possibility. He is righteousness and power. He is perfect love.

His is a love that burns at our core at more than 27 million degrees, simply because He is our God, and we are His people. A holy, light-filled, powerful remnant that lights and leads the way to Jesus.

We have a difference to make and glory to bring to God.

Remember, like Deborah, We have the victory! There is nothing earthly to get or have, only love to be and share, however He authors us to.

"You have stolen my heart, my sister, my bride: you have stolen my heart with one glance of your eyes, with one jewel of your necklace."

- Song of Songs 4:9(NIV)

Nothing makes a woman as unstoppable as pure love. God loves you with a jealous, passionate, unending love. He holds you as close as your next breath, He protects you, guards you, and lifts you up as a light to be seen.

He assures you of victory, reminds you not to be afraid. You are His love, His heart, His very own and He adores you. Walk in the confidence of His love for you. It will set you free, it will cause you to shine His glory and presence, it will lead.

It will lead like the sun, like the Son, and like a girl whose heart is ablaze for the One who makes it all so very worth it. And to whom we sing, "Holy, holy, holy is the Lord God almighty, who was, and is, and is to come!"

"Their line is gone out through all the earth, and their words to the end of the world. In them has He set a tabernacle for the sun."

- Psalm 19:4 (AKJV)

"Oh, magnify the Lord with me, and let us exalt his name together!"

- Psalm 34:3 (ESV)

"Let those who love Him be like the sun, when it comes out in full strength!"

- Judges 5:31 (NKJV)

"Then the righteous will shine forth as the sun in the kingdom of their Father."

- Matthew 13:43 (NKJV)

A Lifetime of Love in Five Days

"Hi Honey, it's mom. I was just wondering if you got my messages earlier today. (there had been two already and it was 10:00 a.m.). Would you call me back, here, at the home? I don't have nothin' and I need you to either come and get me, or pick me up, or bring me my stuff, okay? Please? I need some things and I don't have anything. Thank you, I love you with all my heart, bye."

This was the voice message I received as I headed out the door to go and teach that Tuesday morning, February 2, 2016. I had a full calendar that day and felt a little exasperated that everything was an emergency with my mom, especially if she was out of her favorite brand of popcorn.

I rolled my eyes and sighed as I shook my head realizing that I now needed to stop at the store on my way to work. So that I could stop by the home and drop off her desperately needed items on my way home from work.

"Hi Honey, all I wanted to know is would you please bring with my order, um, get me some Pepsi? Thank you, I love you with all my heart. I will see you in just a little while, bye."

This was the next voice message I received just as I got out of work. I was driving, and on my way to drop off the things I had gotten her before work. Now I would be stopping at the convenience store to get the Pepsi to add to her 'order.'

I was tired and it was cold outside. I grabbed the bags full of her favorites and 'must haves,' in the way of food and personal items, and headed upstairs to room 204 where she stayed. When I got to her room she wasn't there. So I put all of her things away and then headed to the dining room, guessing that is where I would find her. She was sitting with two other ladies eating her dinner. She had her back to me so one of the other ladies pointed out to her that I was there. She quickly turned around and said, "Oh, hi!" and started to get up.

I said, "Mom, don't get up, just eat your dinner."

"No, no, I want to get up. Did you get my things I needed? Do you want me to help you bring them in?" she said, as she hung onto the backs of chairs to be stable on her feet.

"No, I already put everything in your room and I put it away for you, so you are all set," I said.

"Oh, okay, good, thank you. Well, what are you going to do now?" she asked with some exasperation in her voice.

"I am headed home to make dinner and relax. I am pretty tired today," I answered. "You just go back and enjoy your dinner with your friends, and I will see you on Friday, okay?" I said.

"Well, I want to give you a hug," she said reaching out towards me. I stepped towards her and put my arms around her. My fingertips happened to touch the skin on her shoulder. And when they did I heard a voice in my spirit say, 'this is the last cognitive hug you will give her.'

It startled me, and we let go of each other.

She started to turn and head back to her table and I said, "Mom!" She turned back around and looked at me. I said, "I want another hug." She looked at me a little curiously and obliged. As I hugged her my hand touched her skin again, and when it did I heard again, 'this is the last cognitive hug you will give her.' I immediately shrugged it off as me being tired and feeling guilty that I don't do more for her and left.

Day One

Friday, February 5, 2016, at about 10:30 in the morning I got a call from a nurse at the home. "Hi Michelle, I'm just calling to let you know that we have tried several times to get your mom to get out of bed and come to breakfast, but she was not able to respond well. Her right side seems immobile and she is slurring her words, so we are having the ambulance take her to the hospital," she said.

I asked the nurse a few questions to determine the severity of the situation. My mom was prone to small seizures and in and out of the hospital pretty regularly because of them. She seemed uncertain, but repeated that she was being taken to the hospital, and I could find out more there.

I didn't hurry. I sat and finished reading something. I had been through this drill several times in the last few months and I thought; great another day spent sitting in the emergency room. So I didn't hurry. But the longer I sat, the stronger the tug became for me to go to the hospital.

I showered, got ready, and arrived at the emergency room about an hour and a half later. When I walked into her room and I saw her face, something was different this time, and my heart sank into my stomach.

I wanted her to wake up and talk to me so that I could see that this was just another trip to the E.R. and she was going to be fine. I laid my hand on her arm and said, "Mom, mom, can you wake up and see me?" She opened her eyes but they looked hollow and right through me, as if I weren't there. I had never seen her do that before, and I held back tears, trying hard not to look concerned.

My mom has always thought that I am so strong. I have parented her a good portion of her life. I knew if she saw me upset she would worry, so I smiled at her and said, "Mom everything is fine, you have had a stroke. They are taking very good care of you and you are going to be fine. Now just rest, okay?"

I walked just beyond the head of her bed and started to cry. I quickly grabbed some hand towels from the dispenser on the wall and wiped my eyes trying to compose myself. Just then a nurse came in, I think her name was Lisa. She was petite, and exuded sweetness in her hot neon pink trimmed Nike's. She quickly said hello to me and noticing I was upset, asked if I was okay.

Me? Am I okay? Her concern for me caught me off guard. "I'm fine, but can you tell me what the status is with my mom?" I asked. "Has the doctor been in to see her yet?" I questioned anxiously.

Nurse Lisa compassionately replied, "Yes, the doctor has seen her and we have done a cat scan. She has a bleed in her brain that has caused a stroke. They are moving her to the surgical intensive care unit to prepare for a craniotomy."

"So brain surgery?" I asked, as the gravity of the situation and the procedure were hitting me like a tidal wave. This was not another attention-seeking stunt. This was not another routine trip through the E.R.

This was real and scary.

My mind raced to make sense of it, the possible outcomes, and even the idea that I wasn't going to work that day. I stood blank-faced for a moment, digging inside for the resolve to buck-up and become my mom's voice and advocate. All the while harboring a range of emotions I didn't understand.

Lisa answered, "Yes, and we will keep you updated and give you details as we get them. Is there anything you need?"

I replied, "No, thank you, I'm good." She smiled, nodded, and left the room.

The room felt big and cold but filled with a presence that was peace. It was just me and her. She was on the gurney and in my hands, but we weren't alone. This presence hovered and comforted me even as the circumstances were uncertain and unsettling.

I sat down and stared at my mom's face wondering what to do next. I started to pray. I felt helpless. I wanted her to snap out of it, to sit up and be her usual difficult and yet somehow charming self. She is such a fighter, but it felt like her body wasn't letting her fight. She had a helplessness in her eyes I had never seen before. In a panic, I pulled out my phone and began texting my prayer warrior friends, asking them to please pray for her.

Before I knew it, not only were they praying, but my friend Carol was sitting in the chair next to me. She came armed with a beautiful devotional, a warm heart, and a smile that brought much needed comfort.

Watching, Wondering, and Waiting

Mom was shuffled around from the Surgical Intensive Care Unit to the regular Intensive Care Unit. They had decided to see if the medication they had given her would stop the bleed instead of doing surgery. The staff was so apologetic about the moving around, but it gave me hope and peace that this was a good sign, a step down from Surgical Intensive Care.

She got settled, I sat with her for a while, and the doctor and nurses encouraged me to go home. They had another cat scan planned for the early morning to check the bleed in her brain, and they would call immediately if anything changed over night. So I half-heartedly went home, knowing I needed to get some sleep and get my mind around the situation.

I fell into bed that night, hopeful, but exhausted. My head hit the pillow and I was out in no time. The next thing I knew my eyes were wide open and it was about 2:45 a.m. I am a very deep sleeper, so this was not normal for me. I curiously asked God why I was awake like this. I heard in my spirit, 'pray for her.'

So I started praying for my mom. At the same time there was this heaviness on me I couldn't figure out, so I inquired about that too. I asked, "Lord, what is this heaviness that is so on me?" I heard in my spirit, 'a burden for her salvation, pray for her.'

I laid there and continued to pray for her, wondering how I could pray with her. Then I heard in my spirit, 'all you have to do is tell her you are going to pray a prayer, and that if she agrees with the prayer, to simply say, 'yes' in her heart.' I felt relieved and I thought I could manage at least that. I continued to pray for her for about two hours and then drifted off to sleep.

I woke up early the next morning, wanting to get back up to the hospital as quickly as possible. I am not a morning person, so this was not an easy task. As I sat praying and relying heavily on my morning coffee to jump start me and my brain, I received a text message from my friend Carol, who just happens to work at the hospital. She was excited, saying she had been by mom's room, and my mom was sitting up a bit, seeming to be pretty responsive. I was thanking Jesus and Carol, and I was so excited!

Immediately following Carol's text, I'd say less than five minutes, I got a call from the nurse attending to my mom saying she was 'crashing.' They were taking her for a cat scan and the neurosurgeon would be calling me shortly. 'What?'

I flew out of my chair and started getting myself dressed when the neurosurgeon called. "The bleeding is worse, and we want to put a drain in her brain to relieve the pressure, but we need your permission to go ahead," he said.

I asked a few questions about the procedure and then asked, "Will it make a difference for her if I take some time? I need to think and pray about this."

"No, it won't make a difference, but we would like to do it as soon as possible," he said.

"I will be up there in 20 minutes and have an answer for you," I said.

In the car on the way there I felt the same heaviness I had felt during the night come over me again. I began to talk to God out loud, "Lord, I want to pray with her for her salvation, but you will have to give me the courage, the words, and make a way, or I can't do this." I said.

My mind was whirling. I knew I would allow them to do the procedure, at least anything up to the point of intubating her, since I knew this was her wish. I didn't want to make these decisions; I was wrought with emotion, but I knew I had to be strong for her.

As I walked from the parking garage through the hospital lobby I passed face after face, and I was smiling and greeting them. The Holy Spirit was so heavy on me all I could feel was love and compassion for every soul I passed in the corridors. I was wondering what news they had received today, or whom they might have been visiting. This seemed such a strange internal paradox. As I got closer and closer to the ICU, I was so scared to see what I might I see.

I was greeted by a silver haired, gentle man, with glasses. He was soft spoken when he held out his hand and introduced himself as a doctor on my mom's 'team.' Have you ever noticed that as a Christian you can see the 'Christian' on another person? I had no doubt this gentle man was a man of faith and an angel dropped in my path.

He stood beside me, arms folded across his chest, and one finger to his mouth, as in contemplation. "How are you doing?" he asked, as we stood shoulder to shoulder staring at my mom.

"I'm fine, but they tell me the neurosurgeon wants to put a drain in her brain?" I said. "So I guess I am going to have them do that."

"Listen, I want you to know that you are a voice for your mother. You know her wishes, and we do not." He calmly stated: "You are only supporting her in her wishes, so you do not need to feel bad or guilty. Your job is to protect her from us. We will continue to press forward with the next step of care to keep her alive. It is up to you to tell us when she would want us to stop."

With that said, he began to give a status report and possible prognosis, and none of it was good news. He said, "As you go forward, be sure and always ask whatever doctor is taking care of her, what the goal or out-come for any given procedure is meant to be. With that information, you can decide if it is a goal your mom would want."

I thanked him profusely for his time, care, and wisdom. I felt he had equipped me with exactly what I needed to better handle whatever came next.

He left the room after making sure I knew where to find him, and everything went still and quiet. I walked over and sat down in a chair by the window and stared at her face. I thanked God for the sunshine gently gracing the room. And suddenly a strong and peaceful sense hit me that this was the time to pray with my mom. I knew God had cleared the room and made a peaceful space, and it was time for me to pray with her.

I felt glued to the chair and these thoughts filled my mind, 'What do I say, what are the right words, what if she doesn't respond? I can't do this, Lord. I feel so inadequate right now.' I felt utterly frozen in place.

Suddenly, my cell phone began to ring in my purse. 'Who would call me this early? Everyone knows I am never up at this time,' I thought. I answered it, "Hello?" It was my dear friend, Val.

"Michelle, I am on my way to a hair appointment, so I can't talk long, she said. God has given me such a heavy burden for your mom's salvation, I just knew I had to call you and tell you to pray with her." She said with urgency and conviction in her voice.

"Oh my gosh, Val, I said, I can't believe you are saying this right now. I was just sitting here trying to muster the courage to do that. But I am so afraid I won't have the right words or that she won't listen or cooperate."

"Michelle, you have to pray with your mother. You will never be able to live with it if you don't. Satan will try and fill you with doubts and fears. He DOES NOT want you to pray with her. You have to do it now!" She exhorted. "All you have to do is tell her you are going to pray a prayer with her; and if she agrees, she can just say yes in her heart."

'What?' Val had just repeated, almost verbatim, what I heard during the night while I laid awake praying. The spirit instantly rose up inside me after hearing her words and I said, "You're right. I heard the exact same thing last night, Val. I asked God on my way here to make a way, and He has cleared the room. I'm going to do it now. Thank you so much!"

I hung up the phone and took a deep breath. Then I asked God to be with us and to give me the right words to pray. I closed the door to her room and then walked over to her. I shook her gently and said, "Ma, ma."

She opened her eyes a bit and said, "yeah."

"Mom, Do you know who I am?" I asked urgently.

"Yeah," she said.

"Who am I?" I asked. I wanted to be sure she could understand me.

With very slurred words she replied, "Michelle."

I smiled in relief and said, "Yes, mom I want to pray with you right now. Is that okay?"

She said an emphatic, "Yeah."

"Okay," I said, "I am going to say a prayer; and if you agree with the prayer mom, just say yes in your heart, okay?"

Again she said, "Yeah."

I leaned down by her ear, and I prayed the prayer of salvation with her. I asked Jesus to wrap his loving arms around her and that He would hold her close under His wings. I prayed for healing and for His will to be done.

I leaned up and looked at her face and asked, "Mom, did you hear what I prayed?"

She said, "Yes."

"Do you agree with that prayer, mom?" I asked.

"Yup!" she said insistently.

I was flooded with joy and relief. I felt a weight lift off of me that was so heavy, I didn't even know how heavy it was until it was gone. I gently clapped and cried and looked around the room as though there should be someone there to celebrate with us. I wanted to dance, to jump up and down, sing, and praise Jesus. But there we were, with her back to sleep, and me. I decided there was celebration and singing in heaven, so I sat down in the chair again, and stared at her face.

I was flooded with gratitude and awe, but needed to be flooded with coffee. Just then my friend Carol came walking into the room with a very tall coffee. I stood up and started gently clapping again and crying as I walked toward her. She looked inquisitively at me and said, "Is that a happy cry?"

I said, "My mom accepted Jesus."

"Really!" she said, "Oh, how exciting, I'm so happy!"

We rejoiced, and I shared the story with her as we sipped coffee. I could hardly contain my joy and gratitude.

Carol no sooner went back to work when the neurosurgeon came into the room and asked for my decision about the brain drain. I told him to go ahead with the procedure, but asked if she would be in any pain during it, since apparently they do it bedside. I had pictured her going off to the operating room and being given anesthesia.

He assured me that she would only feel a pinch at most. He explained there were no nerve endings once past the insertion point, and they would numb that with a topical anesthetic.

I resolved it in my heart and mind and said, "Okay, I will be in the waiting room." My eyes filled with tears as I headed down the hall. I had the same knot in my stomach as when my son, at three years old, going for a shot at the doctors office asked me, "Mommy is it going to hurt?"

I reached the comfort of the dimly lit waiting room and plopped into a chair. 'I should call family,' I thought. That task felt like a huge burden. Relationships with siblings and relatives are not ideal.

I muddled through each call, explaining the circumstances, and trying to be positive. Just as I was ending my last call, the doctor came in the room. I hung up quickly and asked him how it went.

He explained that he had expected a release of pressure, a possible spurting of blood from the brain, and there wasn't.

"So what does that mean now?" I asked.

"We will be moving her back to the Surgical Intensive Care Unit, in preparation that we may have to do surgery to stop the bleed," He stated.

The question: 'What is happening?' replayed again and again in my mind, like a broken record. Things were going in a direction I didn't want, nor could I control. All I could do was keep saying, "Okay," accepting it, and taking the next step. It felt like I was George Jetson on that treadmill yelling, "Jane, stop this crazy thing!" Mentally and emotionally, I was running to keep up and process everything, but it didn't stop.

My heart ached as I walked back into her room. Her sheet and pillow were stained with iodine. Her hair was shaved where tubes now protruded, and her mouth gapped open as she slept.

'What am I letting them to do you mama, I thought?' Oh dear God I don't want to do this, I don't want to be the responsible one, I cried out in my heart.

Just then the grace-filled, silver-haired, angel of a doctor appeared in the room again. "How are you doing," He asked?

"I'm okay, I just want to make sure I am doing all the right things for her." I sighed.

He acknowledged that she would be transferred to another floor now. He reminded me that everything he told me earlier, the questions he equipped me with, the understanding that I was only fulfilling her wishes, and was her voice and advocate, were still true. He showed me her x-rays and broke down in detail everything that was happening.

I was thanking him again for caring, explaining things, and taking time with me, when Carol came in on a break, with another hug and smile. She probably brought food or drink, I don't remember, but there she was again.

While I was waiting for 'the team' to assemble and transport my mom, a chaplain came in. I believe her name was Rebecca. She asked me if I would like her to pray with my mom. I said, "Please, yes." Then I shared with her how I had prayed with my mom earlier for her salvation. We both got teary-eyed and praised God's goodness.

She said the most beautiful prayer with hands on my mom about how God has seen her whole life. How He followed, pursued, and loved her every day of her life, no matter what she has done. I was so moved and blessed by her loving words spoken over my mom.

When she finished, I thanked her for such a beautiful prayer and words so perfect for my mom. I told her what a tough life my mom had, how our relationship was so strained and often estranged, but how circumstances had brought me to be her primary care-giver for nearly the last year.

She looked me right in my eyes and said, "God knew this was coming, He let you have her for that time, so you both could heal."

I hugged her and sobbed in her arms. The truth in her words, the love, grace, and power of God, and the realization of the love that I now have for my mom, were startling and overwhelming.

The realization and power of that love for her, both God's and mine, girded me with new strength and peace. It instilled a resolve that no matter what the outcome, I would love her with everything I had in me, and I would not leave her side. That if these were her final days or hours, I wouldn't allow her to live one of them without someone beside her who loved her. God had saved her, made her new, and to me she was beautiful and my mom.

Hmmm, I had a revelation, a new sensation really. This is what that mother-daughter feeling must be like. That unexplainable 'thing' I have heard can sometimes exist in that relationship that is so special. The stuff written about in Hallmark cards. A connection, a love, a knowing of one another that words can't name or express, but exists none-the-less.

In the midst of my 'heavy revvy,' the 'transport team' showed up. They unplugged things, heaped things on her bed, hustled around, and as we started to leave the room, I glanced down. There on the window sill was a bean shaped tray with her bottom dentures in them. 'Gross,' I thought, 'I hope someone thinks to bring those.' Please believe I had zero intention of touching that tray, I have a sensitive stomach after all.

No one was getting the tray of teeth, 'Uh, hello, isn't anyone getting these' I questioned in my mind as they all headed for the door. Why is no one looking around for any additional items that she may have left in the overhead compartment? Come on, really? Crap.

I held the tray of teeth, squished into the elevator with three staff members and a gurney, my back pressed against the doors. I struggled not to look down at the dentures in the bean shaped tray, for fear of upchucking all over my mom's feet. 'Oh, you would just think this is a real riot wouldn't you, mom,' I thought, as she lay there peacefully sleeping. It gave me a slight chuckle knowing she really would love it.

Her sense of humor is one of my favorite things about her, she is very funny. She's quick witted with one liners that are often inappropriate, but true; and you can't hep but laugh out loud.

New Life

So on this Saturday evening we were moved up a few floors, physically, spiritually, emotionally, and relationally. And I was settling in for whatever was next. I had decided to sleep at the hospital, in a recliner that didn't really recline beyond 3 inches, but at least had a pop-out foot stool.

My husband came in the evenings bringing me dinner, and a dose of love and logic that I truly needed, amidst the emotional overload. He sat with me, and he brought me clean clothes. He clued me in about how life was happening outside the surreal bubble of that room. My sons popped in and out as their jobs allowed.

Sunday morning came with a heaviness. A family member was coming to visit, and I was very anxious about it. She can be harsh and intense and I can't relate to it. So I prayed a lot and whined to Carol, as she continued to blow in and out, like a refreshing breeze of love and light. Carol stayed with me. My family member came, and it started out as I had anticipated. But I suggested we focus on and talk about what was happening with my mom, and that she was all that was important. She agreed.

So we sat on each side of my mom's bed and talked about family, life, and other random topics. Out of nowhere, I started witnessing to her. I talked about how we don't often think about our after-life until these things happen. But how important it is to think about it all the time. She agreed, but said that her and God would probably fight. I had to laugh. Oh, how I have wrestled with God. I told her that I too wrestled with God, but encouraged her that it is so very worth it.

She leaned in close and talked to my mom. My mom was lifting her eyebrows trying desperately to open her eyes, but she couldn't. Things were left unsaid and unfinished between them, and I knew my mom wanted to see and talk to her so badly. My family member left soon after that. I gave her a hug and told her I loved her, and that I would keep her updated. She lived about two and half hours away.

I did a lot of silly stuff that afternoon. I had one-sided conversations with my mom like, "Hey ma, remember when you took us to Cedar Point when I was around twelve, and you let me drink your tom collins mixed drink on the beach? That was so wrong by the way, but we did have fun." And, "Mom you always loved to dance. Hey, I will dance for you."

I pulled up her favorite Patsy Cline songs on my phone and laid it by her head so she could hear it. Then I danced by her bed, ready to freeze at a moments notice, should the nurse come in. I had warning, because a curtain hung in front of the sliding door, so if it moved I could stop. People do crazy things at times like these, especially me. I believe in fully living whatever moment I am in - even if I look really stupid doing it.

I was also building a new and better relationship with my mom, and I wanted silliness and dancing to be a part of it. So I danced beside her bed as Patsy crooned, "Walking After Midnight." When Patsy finished, I settled back into the recliner that had become 'home.'

All of a sudden beeping, loud obnoxious beeping, was blaring from the monitors and nurses came rushing in. "What is happening," I asked insistently!

"We think her lung has collapsed, and she is not getting enough oxygen," one of them replied. "We are getting a chest x-ray right away."

The x-ray confirmed the lower lobe of her right lung had collapsed. I suddenly had a team of doctors and nurses standing in her room, and as compassionately as possible, asking me for direction. "We can go ahead with intubating her if those are her wishes, or we can put on a forced oxygen mask, or we can do nothing?" They offered.

"She does not want any kind of life support for sure, but how would the forced oxygen help, and what is that like exactly?" I inquired.

"The forced air mask is tightly sealed to her face and forcing oxygen that could potentially re-inflate her lung and that would be our hope," the doctor said.

"Well, then I think that is what we should do," I said.

I stood beside her bed looking at her with this forced air mask on, cuts, stitches, and a tube coming out of the side of her head. Her mouth gapped open and dry. I was so sorry for all she was going through, so guilty like I was doing it to her, or at least allowing it.

I loved her. I loved her and didn't realize how much I did. In my heart I asked God for mercy for her. I couldn't bear to see her suffer anymore. It seemed that the doctor's reports and her condition kept getting worse. So I texted my family members with another update - trying hard to be honest but positive. I wanted to protect them the best that I could.

It felt like a decision point was coming, and I was sick to my stomach about it. I was wrestling inside, praying, begging. I kept thinking of Jesus asking God if this cup could pass Him by and I started asking the same thing.

I didn't want to do be the one to make these decisions. The responsibility felt like it should belong to God, not me. Couldn't He please just take her home right now if it was His will for her? Please? I mean, why include me in the process, I wondered. I was desperate to not be responsible.

My sweet husband arrived with dinner. I was so hungry but could hardly eat. The shift change came for the nurses while we were finishing up dinner. In came a gal, who the moment I saw her I felt connected to her. She asked, "How are you doing tonight?"

"Well," I said, "I guess I have to make some decisions soon and I am feeling anxious."

With that said, she immediately stopped what she was doing, pulled up a chair…yes, pulled up a chair, and sat almost knee to knee with me. She said, "Okay then, let's talk about it. I used to be a hospice nurse so maybe I can help you with the decisions by asking some questions about your mom's status." She then proceeds to make the sign of the cross. Forehead, chest, shoulder, shoulder, the sign of the cross.

'What?' I thought. She asked me questions about the last time she had eaten and other stuff I can't remember but was grateful for at the time. Stuff that allowed me to process things clearly and logically. And then, it was like time froze, and I could only hear her speaking. I heard her say, while making the sign of the cross again, "Don't forget mercy."

Peace fell on me, and in my mind I knew that I was going to have to let my mom go. But I wasn't ready, not today.

As I settled into my recliner to try and get some sleep that night I said, "Hey mom, we're having a sleep over! It's been a long time since we have slept under the same roof. Now don't be snoring I need some sleep." I laughed, as I settled in trying to just have a light-hearted moment with her, while my heart hurt so bad.

Miracles on Monday

I was awakened by the nurses activity around 5:30 a.m. Surprised I had actually gotten a few hours of much needed sleep. They were going to do some kind of scan that morning to see what kind of brain activity was still happening.

Instead, they did a chest x-ray, and other endless checks and tests. This point in the morning was a total blur. The team of doctors showed up, each with a thought or opinion, but none of them had a positive prognosis.

Each conversation I had with them seemed to end with them giving me that squinty face that said, 'I'm trying to say this as gently as possible, but it does not look good.' I asked the female doctor standing next to me to give it to me straight, that I would do better with no beating around the bush.

She said, "She could lay here like this for days or weeks, but she will probably not get any better than this." I already knew the truth of what she said, and it still felt like being punched in the stomach. I swallowed hard and thanked her for telling me.

"The course of action is completely up to you, take as long as you need or want. Maybe you want to contact family out of town, there is no hurry, but we are here to help you however we can." She said.

So, it was either life support, feeding tubes, and the like, or it was removing the forced oxygen mask and letting God and nature take their course. Those were the options. I hadn't even had coffee yet.

She said, "Just let us know when you have decided, and we will go from there."

"I know what to do," I stammered. "I will have you remove the mask, but not yet! I need just a little more time for God to work and me to get my head around this, okay?"

She smiled and said, "Okay, no hurry, you just let us know."

I was happy when they left the room. I needed a moment alone with my mom right then. I bent down by her face and held her hand and whispered, "I don't want to give up on you mom, I know what a fighter you are, but I cannot let you suffer needlessly either. If you are going to fight then fight. But if you are tired and ready to be with Jesus, then go. Don't you dare stay here and just suffer, I mean it. I love you so much so I am putting you, me, and this situation in Gods hands, but it is okay to go if you need to." I kissed her on her cheek and sat back down in my recliner.

I thought, 'oh, I need some coffee so bad dear Lord, if I just had some coffee I might make it through this morning.' I was so depleted. Just then like clouds parting in the sky, the curtain in the doorway was pulled back. There stood Carol, once again, with coffee. Oh, how He loves us.

Carol gave her usual hugs, smile, and hospitality and said she would stop back in a bit, she wasn't quite finished with her shift yet.

Shortly after her leaving, I sat there thinking and praying, feeling a little alone, and incredibly sad. I prayed, "Lord, I just need someone, anyone, I don't even care who, to just sit with me, be by me." Just then my phone rings. I see it is my dear friend Val. I answered it quietly, trying to sound upbeat, "Hello?"

"Hi, Michelle," Val said. "I was just thinking about you and wondering if there is anything I can bring you this morning - if there is anything you need?"

"Oh no, I'm fine. Carol just brought me coffee, and I can't think of anything else I need right now, but thank you," I said.

"Are you sure?" she persisted. "Isn't there anything I can do or bring you?"

"No, no, I don't want you to have to get out, and I am fine, really." I said.

"Ya know," she said. "Would you like me to just come and pray with you?"

What? I thought, this piqued my spirit instantly and I quickly replied, "Yes!" "Yes, I would love that, please."

She chuckled at my sudden change of heart and enthusiastic response and said, "Okay, I will be there shortly then." I thanked her and felt such relief and peace. Valerie has been a mentor in the faith to me, a dear friend, and a sweet sister. She has a nurturing heart and nature straight from God. To have her come there and pray with me felt like a dream come true in that moment.

After about an hour Val, Carol, and I were together in my mom's room. We hugged, I gave an update, and we sat and chatted for a while. I was thanking God and them for the gift of their friendship, and the gifts that each of them brought. When Val took out her bible and sweetly read Psalm 91, of course we cried. It seems God has turned us into bawl babies over the slightest reading of scripture or anything heart-warming for that matter!

When Val finished reading, and we sopped up our tears, Val said, "Well, would you like to pray with your mom?"

I said, "Yes, please."

So the three of us gathered around her bed and laid our hands on her. Val prayed like an angel with anointed words of grace and love. I was soaked in gratitude for Val's prayer and in total joy for my mom. To have these two Godly sisters standing beside me in prayer over my mother was powerful. Words really can't do it justice.

When she finished, we looked up, took a breath, and smiled at each other like a great work had been accomplished, and we weren't even sure exactly what.

We naturally gathered around at the end of her bed and started to talk. I have no recall what about, but Val and Carol were talking to each other while I listened. All of a sudden a strong and deep chill went right through me, and it startled me. I shook hard and felt scared.

Carol noticed me doing this and asked, "What's wrong?"

Then my attention was drawn toward the window to my right, and I started to turn to see what was there. I became so overwhelmed in the spirit. It felt like holy terror. The next thing I know, I was face down over the top of my moms legs on the bed, sobbing so hard it was tough to catch my breath.

Val and Carol were alarmed and wondering what was going on, asking me if I was okay, but I couldn't speak right then.

Somehow I managed to get to my moms face and all I could say was, "Wait till you see how beautiful it is mom, wait till you see!" I sobbed.

I finally was able to collect myself and try to explain what was happening - which was hard because I wasn't completely sure myself. I only knew that something was present and so powerful, I couldn't look at it or stand it.

Carol had an appointment to go to and she left reluctantly. The spirit was so heavy in the room, it was difficult for her to leave. Val offered to pray with me again, and it was perfect and beautiful. As she prayed, the right side of my face felt like someone had taken a heat lamp and held it to my face. I didn't know what was happening My whole right side felt on fire - my face, my arm, and shoulder. After several minutes it faded and stopped. I told Val this was happening as she prayed, and we were both in awe and wonder, praising God.

After Val also reluctantly left, I wondered what do you do after something like that? How does life ever feel, 'normal' again? I sat and looked around the room. I thought about work, and life, and things in general. I noticed how utterly bland everything felt in comparison to that moment. I wondered how life would feel going forward. This was a surreal moment that I wanted to soak in for a very long time.

I was completely spent, yet full of joy, anguish, heart-break, peace, wonder, humility, and profound and complete love. All I knew or wanted to do in that moment was love. It felt like love was all that existed, and the only thing left inside me. It put me on my face and lifted me like nothing earthly is capable of doing.

What, literally, on earth, do I do now after this? I thought.

The slider door slid open and in came my silver-haired doctor friend looking like wisdom and comfort in the flesh. "Hi," he whispered gently "How are you both doing?"

"Good," I said. "I am going to have them remove her oxygen mask, but I am not ready today."

Like a concerned father, he again reiterated how there was no place for me to feel responsible or guilty. He said that I was only carrying out her wishes and that God was in charge of the rest. He said, "You could take her off the mask, and if God wants her here, she will stay. Or you could let her linger for weeks hoping she'll recover; but if He wants her home, He is still going to take her home."

God was bringing me such wisdom, peace, and love through this amazing man and doctor. His words gave me more comfort and resolve that I needed to let her go. It was another step toward getting my mind in alignment with my heart and spirit.

Just then, the door slid open again. Here came three of the nurses from my mom's care home to visit her. They had been calling and getting updates and knew things had taken a turn for the worse. I was so touched they had come.

They started sharing some stories about my mom, and I said, "Yeah, she is a stinker. She likes to break the rules doesn't she?"

They all laughed and said, "Yes she did, but she is a breath of fresh air really. Like the time her and her best friend Pam came walking back up from down the street, walkers and all. We asked them where they had been, that they couldn't just leave without telling anyone where they were going, and they said they were at The International Dog House. They wanted a hot dog for lunch, and they were going to get one!"

I laughed so hard and so did the silver-haired doctor, he said, "I like your mom even more now. What a great spirit she has. I wish I had known her before this."

Just as he said that it occurred to me, she does indeed have quite a spirit. One that often had her saying, "Don't fence me in or hold me down. You'll know I am old when I stop riding roller coasters."

Well, her health didn't let her get on any roller coasters recently, but she still did not want to be held down by anyone or anything. That story those nurses shared reminded me of that fact with renewed clarity. I shared that with the doctor and I said, "She wouldn't even want to be held down by her own body, and that story makes this decision so much easier."

Oh, the Lord is good.

I called for the female doctor on 'the team' that I had spoken to earlier that day. I told her that I would like to take the mask off of my mom the next day. I wanted to give my mom and God room to do whatever they might do, and me one more day to just be with her.

She asked me about what time the next day I thought I wanted to do it so they could prepare the staff and team. I said, "1:00 p.m. Not first thing in the morning, that's just too much, and 1:00 seems like a good time." She agreed and left.

My husband brought dinner again that evening. We sat and watched some mindless t.v. while we ate. My mom laid so still and unresponsive. Every so often I would go over and kiss her cheek or rub her hand.

My body ached so bad from being cold, tense, and sleeping in the recliner. I longed for a bed, a shower, and rest, but it was so worth every ache and pain to be there with her. As I nestled back into that recliner that night, the words of the nurse from the care home replayed in my mind; "She is a breath of fresh air." That felt so novel to hear. Those were not words I had ever heard used to describe my mom. My heart smiled as I tried to close my eyes and get some sleep. I prayed;

"Dear sweet Lord, you know what is coming tomorrow, but if your will is to take her tonight, it is okay with me. I don't want to make this move, so if you want to take her, please do. Please, don't let her suffer Lord, please. I know you love her more than I do. I hate this so much, it is breaking my heart. Please give me the courage and strength Lord, I love you."

Tuesday's Triumph

I actually got a little sleep. I was awakened gently by a nurse who had come in to check on my mom. The intensity and clamor around her care seemed to be glaringly absent. A sense of resignation of what was to come at 1:00 p.m. hung in the air.

I kissed my mom on the cheek and said, "Good morning mama, I love you." I choked back tears and headed for the bathroom to brush my teeth and have a spot bath.

It wasn't long, and Carol came again with coffee and a much needed hug and smile. I told her of the plan to remove the mask at 1:00 p.m. When I did, I started to get really anxious. I was flashing back to watching my dad pass. There was thrashing due to not enough air, color changes in his face, begging with his eyes for help. I could not withstand that again. I was near panic, imagining that this could happen with my mom, when they removed her oxygen mask.

Later that morning, I shared those concerns with the doctors. I told them that when they did remove the mask, I would step out until she was settled and calm. They said, "That's fine, but stay close, because it may not be long after it's removed that she may pass."

I half chuckled, "Oh, you don't know my mom, she will fight to the very end. It won't be too quick."

I just sat with her all morning. Both of my sons came and joined me.

12:00 p.m.

Noon rolled around, I called the nurse in. "Hi, what can I do for you?" she asked.

"I want to move the time we remove her mask to 2:00 p.m. is that okay?" I asked anxiously.

She smiled, "Of course it is. You take all the time you need."

I thought, no, I don't want TOO much more time, but I had cold feet. "No, no 2:00 p.m. will be it, really, I just need a hint more time." I replied. She smiled, nodded, and left the room.

2:00 p.m.

In came 'the team' to remove, well, everything. No more beeping machines, blipping monitors, and sounds of raging oxygen. I bent down by my moms ear and said, "Mom, we are going to get this tight awful mask off of you now, I know it isn't very comfortable, and the nurses are taking very good care of you okay? I love you mom." I kissed her again, and my boys and I stepped into the hallway. Just then my husband arrived, and he was a sight for a desperate heart.

The nurse came out after about 5 minutes. She said there was no reaction, that my mom was calm, and they had given her something to keep her relaxed and free of pain.

I sat on the side of the bed with her and at 7:26 p.m. she passed. We stayed awhile longer and said good-bye. I kissed her again on her cheek and told her I would see her when I got to heaven. "You're free now mom, you're free." I whispered in her ear. Nothing can fence you in or hold you down anymore, I thought, as we headed for the door.

I glanced back at her one more time and walked out of her room for the first time in three days. Since we had all driven separately, I had to drive myself home alone, and I was glad. I remember wailing an ungodly wail of a cry all the way home - a sound I had only heard come from me when my dad had died.

I started begging God and my mom for some sign or reassurance that she was in heaven and with Him. I was exhausted and maybe delirious from it. I was saying, "Mom you always said if I put you in a nursing home you would haunt me. Well, you better at least let me know you are okay. I mean it! I can't stand not knowing how you are. I need assurance mom, I need assurance!" I screamed.

I got home, and I was completely numb with exhaustion. I don't know if my heart or body ached worse. I stood in the shower thanking God for the hot water as it ran over my skin.

I put pajamas on, drew back the covers, and crawled into bed. It felt so good to lay straight, to have warm covers over me, and a soft pillow that I started sobbing in gratitude and drifted off to sleep.

As morning came, just before I really woke up, my eyes were closed and I saw a picture. It was the sky with clouds. The clouds parted in the form of a circle. Looking over the embankment of clouds and down at me was the silhouette of an angel. As I watched it wondering who or what this was, the angel turned side-ways and I could see the outline of its face. I would know that silhouette anywhere. It was my mom.

She was joyous, and she started dancing and suddenly there was another female angel with her. I guessed it to be my grandma. They both were dancing, and I started to hear the lyrics to a song that I just happened across on the internet a month or so before this and had downloaded. I had never heard it before then.

"Blessed assurance, Jesus is mine...this is my story...." I heard. I flashed to being in the car on the way home from the hospital saying, "Mom, I need assurance!"

I literally threw awake, sat straight up, and sobbed. Praise Jesus, I believe I received 'blessed assurance!' Oh, how He loves.

Current culture might expect that I get all kinds of sensitive and careful about people believing in these sorts of things or not before I write them, but that is not what is relevant. The only relevant thing in this entire story is the love of God.

That we might allow ourselves to get out of our heads and our own way, to truly come to know the height, width, breadth, and lengths to which He will go to be our true love.

He will chase you down, lift you up, let you work hard, carry you along, teach you, adore you, never leave you or forsake you. He is a good, good Father.

His love will use you to bring coffee, wisdom, prayers, hugs, grace, shelter, and joy, and turn right around and double bless you for doing the work.

The love of God gave me a life and mother who taught me how to fight for and live the better story God wants to author through me. He wants to do the same through you.

The love of God gave me my mother back, even when I didn't want to take her back or do the work.

The love of God used that time to allow me to heal, to care for and love my mom differently and better, even when I couldn't fully see that that is what was happening.

The love God told me as I gave her one last cognitive hug that it would indeed be the last so I could hug her again.

The love of God woke me in my sleep to pray for my mom's salvation. He literally pursued her to her death bed, He loved her so much.

The love of God gave me exact instructions on how to pray with her for her salvation. And when I got scared and doubt crept in, the love of God sent an obedient friend to give me the encouragement I needed to do it.

The love of God gave me the sweet and most precious gift of praying my mother into His sweet loving arms. Nothing is sweeter than that, nothing.

The love of God brought food, hugs, wisdom, smiles, prayers, and comfort to sustain me, through incredible friends and family.

The love of God was thick and present in that room as I prayed with my friends, and I believe He took her spirit home with Him then.

The love of God provided nurses and doctors and staff so sweet, I often shook my head in disbelief at their kindness and extra efforts.

As long as I live, I will never forget the gifts of love He gave me in so many forms during those five days with my mom. I am forever changed and certain, after living a moment of being literally spent of everything but His love in that hospital room, that His love is all there is and all that matters. The love of God is literally everything.

Our individual worlds, as well as the entire world, need God's people to love well. You are it. You are responsible. You are the light, the hands and feet, the mouth, and the heart of Jesus on this planet. Nothing else matters. Nothing else matters.

I drove by Seymour Street the other day on my way to pick up a relative just out of prison. I tear up every time I pass that street these days. My spirit stirs and moves. I feel Jesus so strongly there. He and I are on to the next faith adventure and storyline. I'm not ready, but I never am. How about you? Are you ready? Let's do this together! Let's clasp metaphoric hands as daughters, sisters, and soldiers, and take another step outward in love and trust.

Love the Lord your God with all your heart, all your soul, all your mind and strength. He will take care of everything else, including you. His love makes you like the sun, when it comes out in full strength, to radiantly lead as light in the world. Go and make disciples of the love of God.

If you do not have a relationship with Jesus Christ and you want to make Him your Lord and Savior. I would like to offer the same prayer to you, that I was blessed to share with my mom. Just pray these simple life-giving words:

Lord Jesus, I want you to be my Lord and Savior. Please forgive me my sins and come into my heart, in Jesus name I pray. Amen

If you prayed this prayer for the first time, you are a new creation in Christ. To further your relationship with Him, get a bible, many people like to use the NIV or New International Version. I use the New King James Version. Google search your local directory for bible believing churches. You may want to visit a few, to find one that feels like a good fit. Pray, and ask God to guide you where He would like you to go. No one there will be perfect, but they will love and support your walk with God, as you get to know Him better.

"That if thou shalt confess with thy mouth the Lord Jesus, and shalt believe in thine heart that God hath raised him from the dead, thou shalt be saved."

- Romans 10:9 (KJV)

"For God so loved the world, that he gave his only begotten son, that whosoever believeth in him should not perish, but have everlasting life."

- John 3:16 (KJV)

"For by grace you have been saved through faith, and that not of yourselves; it is the gift of God."

- Ephesians 2:8 (NKJV)

Jesus loves you, THIS I know, for the Bible tells me so. My prayer, is that you know how much, and lead in it.

Lead Like The Sun Playlist

"Anything worth doing deserves its own soundtrack."

- Michelle Cochran

- All The Way My Savior Leads Me - Chris Tomlin
- Because You Loved Me - Celine Dion
- Brave - Sara Bareilles
- Brighter Than The Sun - Colbie Caillet
- Call On Jesus - Nicole C. Mullen
- Days Of Elijah - Donnie McClurkin
- Do Something - Matthew West
- Ever Be - Bethel Music & Kalley Heilgenthal
- Forever - Bethel Music & Kari Jobe
- Happy - Pharrell Williams
- Here Comes The Sun - The Beatles (Abbey Road)
- Hosanna - Hillsong United
- I Am - Nicole C. Mullen
- I Know that you love me - Martha Munuzzi
- I'm Coming Out - Diana Ross
- I'm Free - Kenny Loggins
- In Over My Head - Bethel Music
- Isaiah 58 - Urban Doxology
- Jesus, We Love You - Bethel Music & Paul McClure
- Joy Medley - Yolanda Adams
- Just Might Change Your Life - Sidewalk Prophets

- Learning To Be The Light - New World Son
- Little Bird - Misty Edwards
- A Little Longer - Bethel Music & Jenn Johnson - I listened over & over....
- Lord I Need You - Chris Tomlin
- Love Come To Life - Big Daddy Weave
- Love Overboard - Gladys Knight & The Pips
- The Main Event - Barbara Streisand
- Oceans - Hillsong United
- Oh Happy Day - Bebe Winans
- So Small - Carrie Underwood
- Speak Life - Toby Mac
- Stronger - Mandisa
- Teach Me - Nicole C. Mullen
- This Is Amazing Grace - Phil Wickman
- This Is It - Kenny Loggins
- This This - Nicole C. Mullen
- Walking On Sunshine - Katrina & The Waves
- You Are My One Thing - Bethel Music & Amanda Cook

These are the songs that ministered to me as I wrote this book and I am excited to share them with you. Because every story, project, or piece of art created, deserves a soundtrack. I hope it blesses and encourages you as you listen to it.

Music is so powerful. It has been a tool I have used to minister to me my entire life. It moves us like nothing else can. It can take us back to a specific moment in time or place and I believe it can do the same thing in moving us forward.

When I begin a new project or even season in my life, or I have a dream or vision for my future. I create a playlist for it. I find that as I listen to what sounds to me like the next step in my story, it pulls me forward.

I encourage you to do the same thing. Make a playlist for whatever God is talking to you about right now, or where you believe He is leading you to next. Listen to it regularly and see what happens.

Its fun, effective, and when you reach where you are going, you will have a great keepsake of music, for remembering your journey to the new place in your story.

Note About This Project

This book had been brewing and evolving inside me for a while. I sat one morning in quiet wonder with God in prayer, and I asked Him, "God what is this thing you want to create through me?"

Suddenly I began to hear this 'download' of words to the tune of "What Child Is This." This is what I heard:

What tool is this you will create to serve a generation?
A book, a guide, a ray of hope that brings some inspiration?

To lead, to lead, it's what we need, a church on fire for Jesus.
To lead, to lead, because we know, this world is not long to keep us.

Let's leave behind a legacy that glorifies our Father.
To live in flesh or for ourselves would not be worth the bother.

To lead, to lead, it's our great call, in Christ we rule and reign.
To lead, to lead, as love and light that the lost will be found again.

Thank Jesus, praise Jesus for He is our Savior and Light.
Thank Jesus, praise Jesus we walk on in His glorious might.

To lead, to lead, it's what we need, a church on fire for Jesus.

To lead, to lead, because we know, this world is not long to keep us.

I thought it was random, fun, and worth sharing. I hope you enjoyed it and sang along.

Authors Page/
What Others Have To Say

Michelle Cochran is a passionate leader following God's call on her life to catalyze this generation to live in the freedom of letting go of perfection to lead effectively. Through Michelle's personal journey of faith, she shares her own experience honestly, and gives practical and inspirational guidance to other women who desire the freedom of a God-filled life.

Michelle is a perceptive and sensitive woman whose spirit is one of encouragement and support. Through our personal and business relationships I found that Michelle is the consummate cheerleader for all women to reach their dreams, live contentedly and full of faith. For those of you who struggle with perfection and balancing everyday life with your spiritual walk. Take encouragement from Michelle's example, if you want to grow spiritually while you are discovering who you really are in Him.

Jane Robinson, Artist, &
Director of The Reading Writing Connection
(moxy marketplace) www.moxymarketplace.com

I have known Michelle Cochran for a few short years now, but it feels like forever. I first met her when she attended a Bible Study I was leading in my home. It became apparent very early on that she had a hunger and thirst for God and a deep longing for a sincere relationship with Him. After the Bible study was finished she asked me if I would be willing to mentor her and so our journey began. She soon became one of my closest friends. Our spirits had the same longing for Jesus and we could spend hours talking of Him and the work we saw Him doing in our lives and those of others. We also knew He had called us out to do His work for the Kingdom. I vividly remember when Michelle knew without a shadow of a doubt that God was calling her to write. We were at a Storyline conference in Chicago. That night in our hotel room she began to cry tears of joy as she told me that she now knew what the angst in her soul for months was all about. God was calling her to write.

Her story is the one that God called her to write. It shares the redemptive work of Christ in her own life and the light of Jesus with all who have open hearts to receive it for their own. Her life has been one of hardship, loss, rejection, and abandonment, yet she has been sought out, healed, loved, and redeemed by a Savior who will now use her story to reach the lost for Him.

I am so excited that Michelle has written her story to share with the world and I wait expectantly to see God use it for His glory.

Valerie Hunsberger
Women's Bible Study Leader
facebook.com/daughtersofzionarise

"Michelle and I have been friends for a long time but the last two years have brought us very close during our walk with Jesus. She has grown in her faith in leaps and bounds. I have been inspired by her love & obedience to God. She is an amazing writer & uses her life experiences to encourage others. She truly is a great leader, teacher, & friend."

Carol Greer
A sister in Christ

"Michelle has been my coach for eight years. Her beliefs, perspective, guidance, wisdom, language, and love have been the wind beneath my wings and the number one thing keeping me going so I can serve others – a match made in Heaven."

Nancy Rizzo
Certified Life & Wellness Coach
www.nancyrizzo.com

Michelle Cochran is a writer and personal development coach. She believes every life is a storyline God authors for leadership. She loves deep conversations, hard laughter, and gatherings that cultivate faith, courage, and potential. She is founder and editor of Ladies Who Lead Magazine. She is co-author of the #1 Amazon Best-Seller: Align, Expand, and Succeed. Her Blog is called Strong Girl Productions. She lives in Michigan with her husband Mark, she has three adult children, one grandson, and an unruly passion for Jesus.

To Connect With Michelle:

Email: michelle@stronggirlproductions.com
Blog: www.stronggirlproductions.com
facebook.com/stronggirlproductions
twiiter.com/StrongGirlProd
pinterest.com/StrongGirlProd

Printed in the United States
By Bookmasters